Addressing Loss of Belief in the Real Presence

What we can do as a parish and as an individual
to better restore belief in
and evangelize Christ's Eucharistic Presence

Rich May

While an ecclesiastical approval was not requested nor received, this publication has been through two diocesan reviews, and the recommended changes were incorporated into the manuscript.

En Route Books and Media, LLC
5705 Rhodes Avenue
St. Louis, MO 63109

Contact us at contact@enroutebooksandmedia.com

Cover Photo Credit: Allison Girone
With Permission

ISBN-979-8-88870-443-1
Library of Congress Control Number: Available at https://catalog.loc.gov

Acknowledgements

Author Dr. Peter Kwasniewski

While in residence in the guest house at EWTN, I had the opportunity to review Dr. Kwasniewski's excellent book *The Holy Bread of Eternal Life.* It has been a valuable resource for putting this material together. My thanks for his encouragement.

Troy Guy

Troy Guy is a nuclear scientist, a convert to Catholicism and a dynamic popular national speaker. Troy is the Author of *The Evangelical Catholic.* He is an astute apologist appearing on EWTN and other Catholic radio programs.

Editorial Team

There have been contributions by a number of key people. These include the clergy and those experienced in religious education. Special mention: Joan Barros, Barbara Visser, Tammy Baldauff, and Shirley Weaver.

A very special thanks to Linda Bentzen, whose prior experience with a publisher was extremely valuable in the final editing of the manuscript.

About the Author Rich May

Author of ***Addressing Moral Confusion,*** Rich May is a former Air Force pilot and a retired aerospace engineer by profession. He has a BA in Pastoral Theology from the University of St. Thomas in Houston and an MA in Theology and Christian Ministry from the Franciscan University in Steubenville Ohio. He has appeared several times on the Eternal Word Television Network (EWTN), often on Catholic radio, and for four years hosted a live weekly show on Radio Maria. With an approbation from the Archdiocese of Galveston-Houston, he speaks locally and nationally. Rich has 38 years experience teaching catechesis at all levels and has authored several booklets including *The Rosary a Prayer For All Christians* and *The Rosary a Prayer for All Native Peoples.*

What they are saying about *Addressing Loss of Belief in the Real Presence …*

Rich May offers here a well-formed plan to restore belief in the true and real presence of the Lord in the Holy Eucharist. It combines Scriptural and doctrinal teaching with practices and piety necessary to manifest our belief. And here is a great strength of this book since it challenges us to restore many pious and liturgical practices that were sadly discarded over the last fifty years in most of our parishes. So here is a plan both doctrinal and practical! A must read for all parish leaders and every Catholic. -- **Msgr. Charles Pope, Archdiocese of Washington, D.C.**

I found no doctrinal error in the book. It represents a faithful, traditional, and well-documented call for greater reverence, better catechesis, and liturgical renewal, fully within the bounds of Catholic orthodoxy. It offers faithful, orthodox, and pastorally grounded reflections consistent with the teaching of the Catholic Church, in my humble opinion. Thank you very much for doing this! So much needed in our times!!
Catholic Priest

The Eucharist is the source and summit of our Christian faith and life. It is central to our identity as Catholics, because it is the greatest treasure we have. The Eucharist is heaven on earth! This is why it is so alarming to see a continual decline and loss in the belief in the Real Presence of Jesus Christ in the Eucharist by many who profess to be Catholics. Rich May presents not only a practical way in which we can address this crisis of faith, but also profound and sound theology to help us better understand why it is we do what we do, why gestures and external attitudes also play a pivotal role in professing to the world our belief that Jesus is truly and really present in the Most Holy Eucharist. The profession of our faith in the Real Presence matters more than ever, especially in a world that is so wounded by moral relativism and seeks the light and fullness of Truth, which we can only find in Jesus Christ and His Church. I highly recommend reading this book and implementing its action points. **Catholic Priest.**

Not every change is good. The change that brings about loss of faith is definitely not helpful. This book points out some innovations going on within some local churches that draw members away from the faith. The book succinctly calls for a return to the practices that first gave the church its identity and distinctive taste. I strongly recommend it to be widely read, taught and applied. **Catholic Priest.**

In this book, Rich May offers many fine points and draws upon important sources. He provides some concrete suggestions for addressing the tragic decline of belief in the Eucharist as the true Body, Blood, Soul and Divinity of Jesus Christ. Even those who might not agree with all his suggestions will appreciate Rich's zeal for increased reverence towards the Holy Eucharist. This book is written with a passionate love for the sacrifice of the Mass and the precious gift of Holy Communion. **Robert Fastiggi, PhD, Professor of Dogmatic Theology, Sacred Heart Major Seminary, Detroit, Michigan,**

As a Catholic school principal, I find Rich May's work invaluable for addressing the decline in Eucharistic belief, providing practical recommendations that will help cultivate a profound appreciation for the true presence and the rich traditions vital for the Church's future. **Catholic School Principal**

Rich May's book on a *Addressing Loss of Belief in the Real Presence* is not to be missed by any Catholic who has the opportunity to read it! I thought I was pretty well informed but in my reading I came away with so much knowledge of how we got to where we are (on belief in The Real Presence). I feel that this material will return the laity to a true love for Jesus in the Eucharist, which, in turn, will lead to greater attendance at Mass and more vocations to the priesthood. **Former ACTS Core Team**

Rich May's book is a rich resource in Eucharistic belief and practice that will help parishes understand the need for deeper faith in, and greater reverence for, Christ in the Holy Eucharist and the practical means of bringing those about.
Former Parish Faith Formation Director

In his book, *Addressing Loss of Belief in the Real Presence,* Rich May hits at the heart of the reason for the decline of reverence and belief in the True Presence happening in our churches today. Every pastor needs to read this book! **Retired catechist and teen mentor**

I started receiving the Eucharist on my tongue a year ago. This book on a Post Eucharistic Revival reinforced the wisdom of traditional reception of His Real Presence. Reading about the early Church teachings and practices opened up once again the mystery I felt as a young child just beginning to receive God in my own body. I am so grateful for this book.
Retired Teacher

"Addressing Loss of Belief in the Real Presence" is a thoughtful and thought-provoking book with a thorough treatment of the topic from both historical and spiritual perspectives. It is a compelling argument for change. **Long time OCIA Catechist.**

Rich May has written a powerful book on a subject critical to all Catholics; the Eucharist. It is an easy read which makes the complicated theology understandable and a very practical explanation of why it is so important to get the Eucharist right. **Former: Chairman of the Board Christian Renewal Center, Chapter Director, ACTS Missions**

As a youth director, Rich May's *Addressing Loss of Belief in the Real Presence* is an extremely helpful tool. Teens seriously lack a proper understanding of the Eucharist, but this is not entirely their fault. The parishes they are growing up in, for whatever reason, water the Faith down so as to try to "meet them where they're at." This approach has been a disaster. In this book, Rich May does what not too many Catholics are willing to do and calls out the elephant in the room. Addressing the topics of music, dress and reception of the Blessed Sacrament, Rich provides a sound and orthodox analysis -- and he does so while remaining faithful to the Magisterium of the Church. Teens do not reject the Church's teaching about the Eucharist solely because of insufficient catechesis; rather, they reject it because adults treat the Eucharist as if it is just a symbol. If every parent in a diocese read this book, a true Eucharistic revival would happen quickly. **Parish Youth Director**

Saint Joseph Catholic Church, Cleveland, Oklahoma. Photo by Rich May

Contents

Dedicated to the two women in my life, my spiritual mother in Heaven, the Blessed Virgin Mary, and to my earthly love and blessing in my life, Cynthia.

True Wisdom

An ascent to the Truth,
encompassed by faith.
A labor of love,
nurtured by grace,
tempered with obedience,
received in prayer,
bathed in the light of the Spirit,
always through Mary.

Rich May

"My friend, if Jesus stood in front of you now, you would kneel, believe me, you'd put your face right on the ground, because suddenly you would know the awesome presence of God."

Mother Angelica

The Church in our times has the urgent need of courageous voices and defense of the greatest treasure, which is the mystery of the Eucharist. Often today, there arise voices in defense of the many human and temporal needs, but rare are the voices that defend the Eucharistic Jesus.

Auxiliary Bishop, Athanasius Schneider

Preface

It is the common opinion of many, this author included, that the greatest crisis in the Church today is the desacralization of our Lord in the Holy Sacrifice of the Mass, that is … the loss and the sense of the sacred and the loss of reverence contributing to loss of belief in the Real Presence.

For too long, as various surveys and statistics have indicated, we have witnessed a decline of belief in the Real Presence, and … in the *sense of the sacred,* in the sacredness of how we honor Christ in the Eucharist.

Many feel that something is missing, namely, a sense of reverence, especially in the way we *receive* the Body, Blood, Soul and Divinity of Jesus Christ in Holy Communion. The unsettling reality is that many Catholics today even though regularly attending Mass, no longer believe the Eucharist is the Body and Blood of Jesus Christ. Countless generations have believed that the Eucharist is the *source and summit of the Christian life* ... the *spiritual heart of the Church* you might say.

This is not just a statistic. It is a crisis of faith!
How did we get to this point?

One solution may rest in returning to many of the traditions and liturgical practices that were part of the Church for over 1500 years. A loss in belief in the Real Presence was never a concern up until the mid 20th century.

This author is not the only one who feels this way. Many in the Catholic press, the clergy, theologians and the laity concur. In 2021 the USCCB responded, organizing a three year Eucharistic Revival, with its principal goal to *restore belief in the Real Presence.*

Such is the focus of this book, not only in briefly touching on what was accomplished in the three year revival, but also what was not addressed and what we can do to make this revival more successful. I don't believe the revival ended in 2004. The revival must continue. It has to continue. It must be an ongoing effort. The Author.

O Most Holy Trinity,
Father, Son, and Holy Spirit,
I adore you profoundly.
I offer you the most precious
Body, Blood, Soul,
and Divinity of Jesus Christ
present in all the tabernacles of the world,
in reparation for the outrages, sacrileges,
and indifference by which He is offended.
By the infinite merits of the Sacred Heart of Jesus,
in union with the Immaculate Heart of Mary,
I beg of you the conversion of poor sinners.

My God,
I believe, I adore, I hope, and I love thee;
I ask pardon of you for those
who do not believe,
do not adore, do not hope, and do not love thee.

Photo by Rich May in the Culinary Institute of America, Hyde Park, New York. In what once was the main sanctuary of a Jesuit Seminary and now is a cafeteria, students receive secular food where once people received supernatural food, the Bread of Angels.

USCCB Revival Prayer

***Lord Jesus Christ, you give us your flesh and blood for the life of the world, and you desire that all people come to the Supper of the Sacrifice of the Lamb. Renew in your Church the truth, beauty, and goodness contained in the Most Blessed Eucharist.
Jesus living in the Eucharist, come and live in me.
Jesus healing in the Eucharist, come and heal me.
Jesus sacrificing yourself in the Eucharist,
come and suffer in me.***

***Jesus rising in the Eucharist, come and rise to new life in me.
Jesus loving in the Eucharist, come and love in me.
Lord Jesus Christ, through the paschal mystery of your death and resurrection made present in every Holy Mass, pour out your healing love on your Church and on our world. Grant that as we lift you up during this time of Eucharistic Revival, your Holy Spirit may draw all people to join us at this Banquet of Life. You live and reign with the Father
and the Holy Spirit,
God forever and ever.
Amen.***

Our Lady of Guadalupe, Mother of the Eucharist,

Pray for us.

Introduction

As we review factors that have led to a loss of belief in the Real Presence, our starting point has to be the three year Eucharistic Revival by the United States Conference of Catholic Bishops (USCCB). Their stated goal:[1]

The 2021-2024 strategic plan for the United States Conference of Catholic Bishops (USCCB) centered on the theme "Created Anew by the Body and Blood of Christ, Source of our Healing and Hope" and a key priority of this plan focuses on a National Eucharistic Revival with the overarching goal of enkindling a living relationship with the Lord Jesus Christ in the Holy Eucharist AND ***reinforcing our belief in the REAL PRESENCE*** *which statistically shows it had dropped well below 50%, even to the 30% level.*

The Revival had a strategic three-year focus ...

Year One (June 2022-June 2023) was a *Year of Diocesan Revival* with events that included Eucharistic Congresses and designated days for formation and reflection.

Year Two (June 2023-June 2024) was the *Year of Parish Revival* that included catechetical formation and extended opportunities for Adoration and Reconciliation.

Year Three was the *Year of the National Eucharistic Congress* July 17-21, 2024 in Indianapolis, IN.

Two Surveys of Interest

2019 PEW Foundation[2]

The USCCB acknowledged the troubling 2019 Pew Research Study which indicated that 70% of Catholics don't believe in the Real Presence. Now you might say ... well, those Catholics probably don't go to Mass or are fallen away Catholics. Not so:

Those who no longer believe but attend Mass ... 50%

Those under 40 who no longer believe (including the youth) but attend Mass… 80% !

While one can dispute the exact percentages or criteria, the survey data is still concerning.

What is interesting is that many of the people who don't believe in the Real Presence know what the Church teaches on the Eucharist. **They <u>know</u> that the Church teaches it is the Body, Blood, Soul, and Divinity of Jesus Christ.** ***Yet they still don't believe.*** And so reliance on catechesis alone, which one would think would solve the problem, is not enough. There must be another element or aspect of all this that we are missing. Why don't they believe? Keep this in mind as we proceed.

The July 2024 *Real Presence Coalition* (RPC) survey

This survey was extensively covered in the Catholic press,[3] and note that it was the largest survey of U.S. Catholics ever conducted. It received nearly 16,000 responses including 14,725 U.S. lay Catholics across every Latin diocese in the country with 780 responses submitted by attendees of the U.S. Bishops National Congress in Indianapolis. Surveys from organizations such as the Pew Foundation and Center for Applied Research in the Apostolate (CARA) come nowhere close to the number of Catholics participating in this survey. The RPC survey drew heavily upon practicing Catholics with 97% of respondents saying they attend Mass at least once a week and believe in the Real Presence, 84% identified themselves as Catholics from infancy.

The RPC survey asked what has contributed most to the loss of faith in the Eucharist. The overwhelming response was the reception of *Holy Communion in the hand while standing* … 58% said it had the greatest level of impact. The majority also mentioned the use of extraordinary eucharistic ministers, replacement of sacred music with contemporary music, loss of silence, ending *ad orientem* worship (facing forward, east), the removal of altar rails, and failure to hold Adoration and eucharistic processions more frequently. In short, the faithful want reverent, solemn worship, and an end to these various liturgical practices which have contributed to the loss in belief in the Real Presence, and the restoration of the more traditional liturgical practices. Are they right?

When and how did Communion in the hand start?
What role did Vatican II play?
What difference does it make if in the hand or the tongue?
What is it specifically about these current practices that erodes belief in the Real Presence?

These are just a few of the issues that need to be discussed and also provide some guidelines and suggestions that we can do as part of our ongoing Eucharistic Revival.

---

1 USCCB National Revival Website https://www.eucharisticrevival.org/press-releases/usccbs-national-eucharistic-revival-prepares-for-highly-anticipated-launch-during-feast-of-corpus-christi. Accessed July 25, 2025.

2 2019 Pew Survey https://www.eucharisticrevival.org/press-releases/usccbs-national-eucharistic-revival-prepares-for-highly-anticipated-launch-during-feast-of-corpus-christi. Accessed April 25, 2020.

3 National Catholic Register, LifeSiteNews, others.

Literature Available

The USCCB

There are several publications and commentaries on what this revival should look like. As of 2025, they are still available online and via the USCCB. *The National Eucharistic Revival, Christ Always With Us* can be downloaded. For our purposes, they have been used to identify the chief goals and objectives which we will briefly review and draw upon during the courseof this effort to identify the problem.

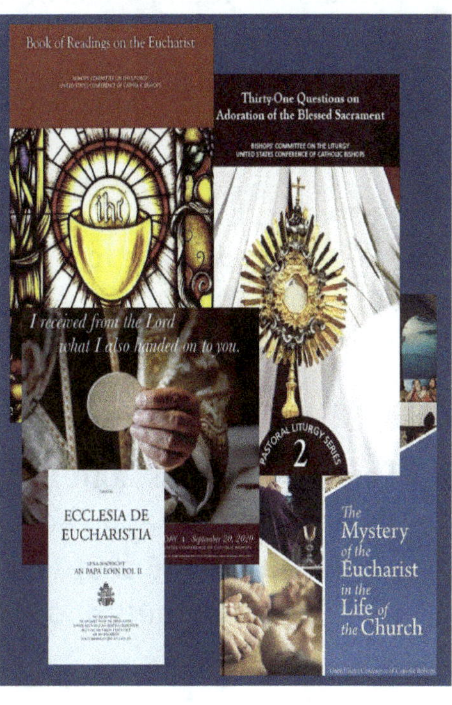

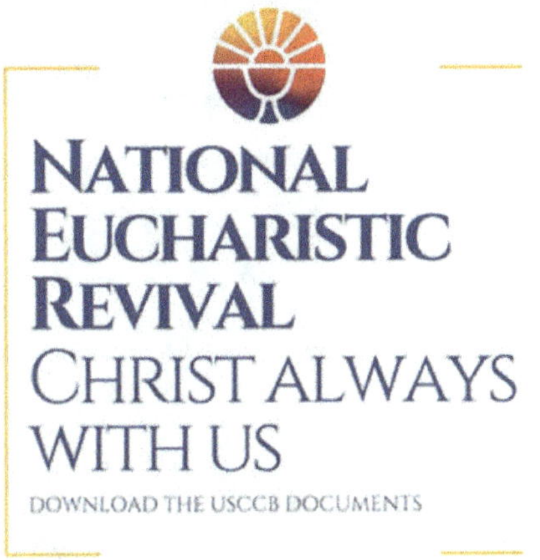

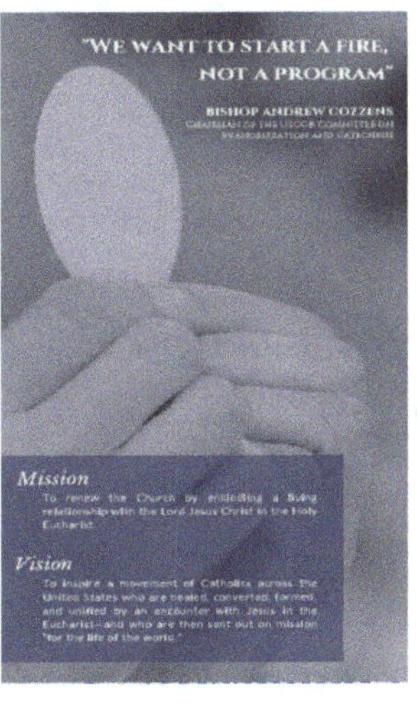

Four additional sources of information will be cited as well (see Bibliography). They are works by notable authors covering the topics discussed. Perhaps most significant is the work *The Holy Bread of Eternal Life* by Dr. Peter Kwasniewski. It is highly recommended, and deals directly with the issues we face, drawing from Scriptures, the Fathers of the Church and the Magisterium. It also discusses what is at stake regarding belief in the Real Presence. Post Vatican II liturgical developments are covered particularly well by Rev. Rodolfo Laise.

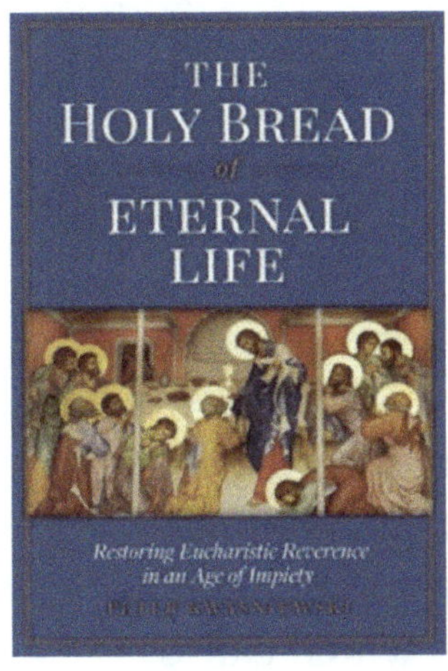

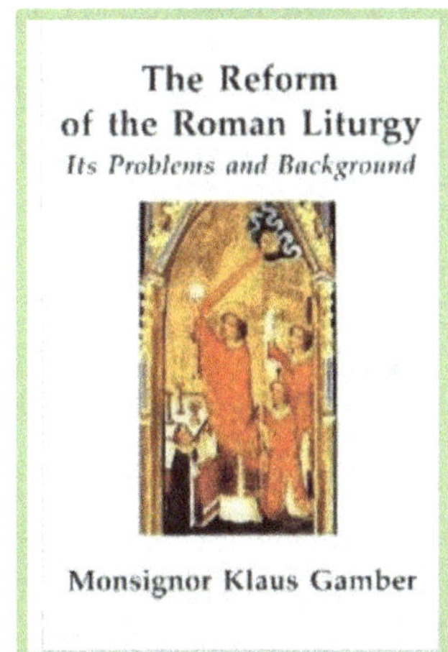

The Five Pillars of the Revival [4]

Depending how you organize the material, the USCCB has identified either four or five "pillars" or foundations of the revival. For the purposes of this work, the five pillars will be used and referred to in the chapters to follow, especially pillars four and five. Just briefly they are ...

PILLAR ONE

Fostering Encounters with Jesus through the Eucharist

We can encounter Jesus in the Eucharist not only through Communion, but also in Eucharistic Adoration. Adoring and encouraging others to adore the Most Blessed Sacrament is essential.

PILLAR TWO

Truth, Goodness, and Beauty of the Eucharist

Plato, Aristotle, and Thomas Aquinas taught that God is truth, goodness and beauty. The Bishops highlight this ... and include *the Truth of our teaching and beauty of our worship ...*

So the Real Presence is not just another Church teaching. but the very embodiment of truth, goodness, and beauty, reflected in beautiful churches, worship at beautiful Masses with beautiful music, and … beautiful prayers and homilies.

PILLAR THREE

Empower Grassroots Creativity

"Empower grassroots creativity by partnering with movements, apostolates, parishes, and educational institutions." Interestingly enough, they mention the principle of subsidiarity, pointing out the importance of small communities. They include the pro-life movement, the Traditional Latin Mass movement, the Catholic charismatic movement, and stressed:

We don't shut off the views and practices of our community that may be involved in a movement that, in fact, supports a great love for the Eucharist.

PILLAR FOUR

Reach the smallest unit: parish small groups and families

… where a person's faith is born and sustained. They rightly mention the use of sacramentals and other practices and devotions that have been forgotten or fallen into disuse such as the Rosary, the miraculous medal (where are the novenas today in honor of the miraculous medal?) and scapulars that bring back fond memories which causes to fall in love once again with our faith and can lead to conversions.

Pillar Four is very important ...because it relates directly to the issues and practices we have today, especially regarding the reception of Holy Communion.

They recognize the <u>importance of the optics</u> ...

... using a specific example like genuflecting before the tabernacle as a way of outwardly starting conversations and is a visual witness, visually to others of what we believe. In short...

It's not enough to believe we must <u>act</u> like we believe. Externals matter. Actions speak louder than words!

We will refer to Pillar Four often.

PILLAR FIVE

Embrace and learn from the various rich eucharistic traditions ...

Adoration, Holy Hour, Benediction, eucharistic processions are just a few of the many traditions that unite Catholics through the Blessed Sacrament, as is the importance of placing the tabernacle containing the Eucharist in the center of the church or in "a distinguished place" (per Can. 938).

And:

Appropriate reverence during the act of receiving Holy Communion.

The USCCB mentions that appropriate reverence during the act of receiving Holy Communion is standing or kneeling, in the hand or on the tongue; all are ***<u>acceptable</u>*.**

Could this be a concern as the surveys indicate?

Acceptability is the daughter of minimalism.

Do we need to move beyond "acceptable" and instead embrace "appropriate?"

Is one of the approved body postures by the Church more *appropriate* of the two? This is another area that needs to be addressed.

In summary, certainly there are a lot of positives in the USCCB approach. Keep these five pillars in mind, and we will refer to them moving forward as we develop *our own perspective on this problem of loss of belief in the Real Presence.*

How well did we address some of these during the 3 year Revival? Is there more that we can do?

---

4 USCCB National Revival Links: https://catholic-link.org/pillars-national-eucharistic-revival-usccb/. Accessed June 14, 2023.

Topics to be discussed

This pie chart diagram is divided into some of the key areas that need to be addressed that impact belief in the Real Presence – and an approximation of their relative importance. While one could argue the relative importance, they all play an important part and therefore are worthy of discussion.

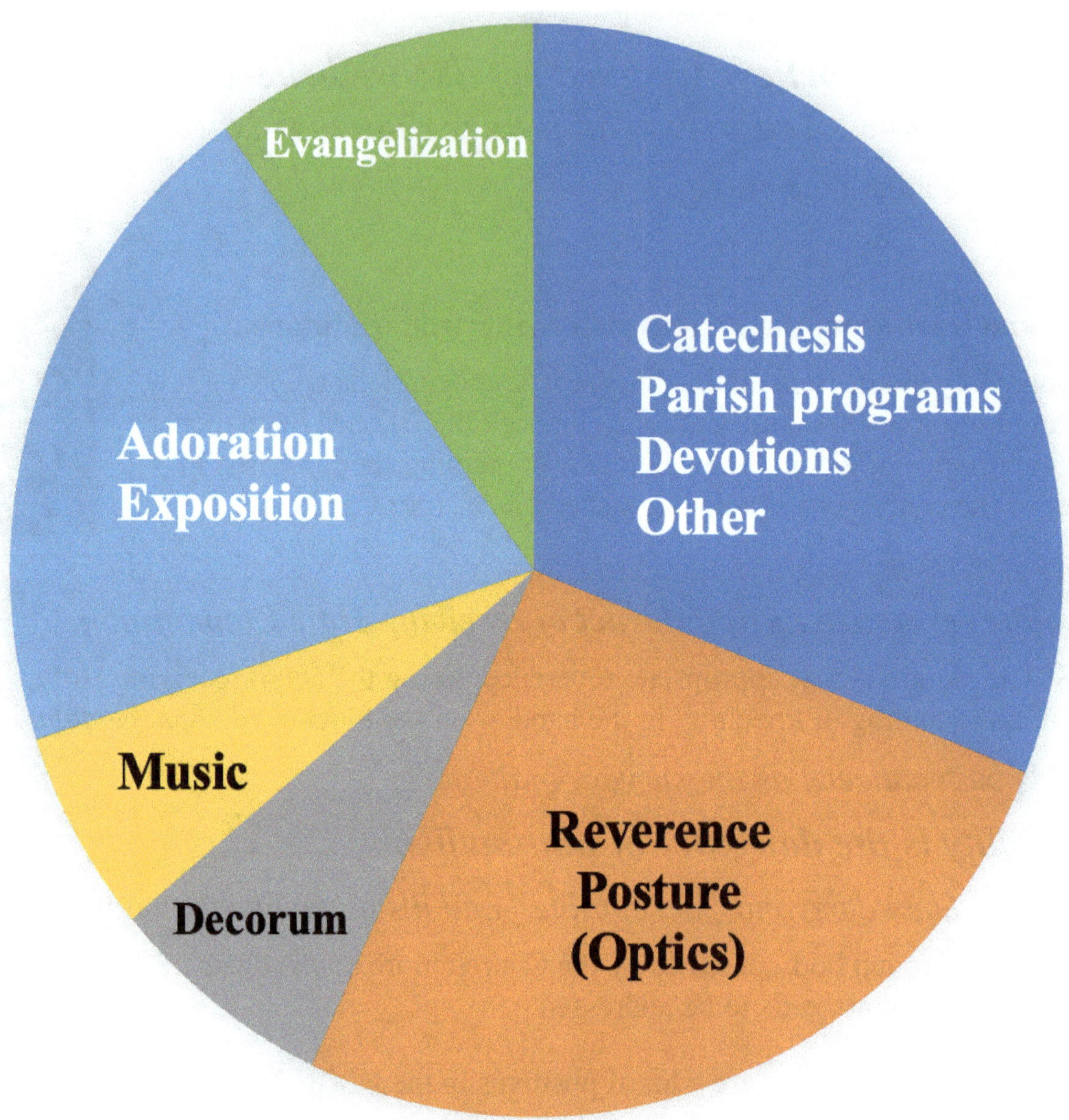

Factors Impacting Belief in the Real Presence
by Rich May

There are issues on the chart mentioned by the USCCB but need to addressed further, especially in the light of the Catholic press and the RPC survey. So lets get started.

It's not enough to believe – we must act like we believe!

Robert Montgomery

Actions speak louder than words!

Prayer by St. John Henry Cardinal Newman

I place myself in the presence of Him, in whose Incarnate Presence I am before, I place myself there. I adore You, O my Savior, present here as God and as Man, in Soul and in Body, in true Flesh and Blood. I acknowledge and confess that I kneel before that Sacred Humanity, which was conceived in Mary's womb, and lay in Mary's bosom; which grew up to man's estate, and by the Sea of Galilee called the Twelve, wrought miracles, and spoke words of wisdom and peace; which in due season hung on the Cross, lay in the tomb, rose from the dead, and now reigns in heaven. I praise, and bless, and give myself wholly to Him, Who is the true Bread of my soul, and my everlasting joy.

Amen.

Chapter 1 Catechesis

A Root Cause

As statistics have shown, many people know the Church's teaching on the Real Presence, *but they still do not believe.* Sufficient sacramental catechesis clearly has to be a starting point and there are ways we can strengthen our catechesis to explain WHY we believe in the Real Presence. It's not just WHAT we believe. It's WHY we believe. It's not just an ideology. The Catechism of the Catholic Church (CCC) should be an important resource.

In the words of Pope St. John Paul II, in his encyclical on the Eucharist... *Ecclesia de Eucharistia,* (n.1) ...

The Eucharist is "the source and summit of the Christian life" --"The other sacraments, and indeed all ecclesiastical ministries and works of the apostolate, are bound up with the Eucharist and are oriented toward it. For in the blessed Eucharist is contained the whole spiritual good of the Church, namely Christ himself" [and] it is *"the sum and summary of our faith"* (CCC 1324).

Let's think about this -- think of the sacraments we have - Penance/Reconciliation – why do we go to this sacrament? One reason is so that we can most perfectly receive Eucharist, so we can be in the state of grace. Also ... the sacrament of Baptism -- as we become members of the Christian community -- and ultimately share in the Eucharist, which binds us together.

So the Eucharist is central to the faith! Loss in our belief in the True Presence has serious consequences.

The decline in our eucharistic devotions has several causes. Primarily, it is due to **rationalism** – that the human mind can understand everything that is perceived by the senses; that our minds are the measure of everything in heaven and on earth, of what Jesus knew or did not know.

We hear too:
"Well I don't know how Christ can be in a piece of Bread."
I don't know how God made the world!!
He made himself into man – why can't He make bread into himself!

There are still natural mysteries we can't explain all around us.
Well – there are *supernatural* mysteries too.

As the heavens are lifted up above the earth, so are my thoughts lifted above your thoughts, or – as St. Paul writes (Rom 11:33):

Oh the depths of the riches of the wisdom and knowledge of God, how incomprehensible are his judgments and his unspeakable His ways, for who has known the mind of the Lord.

The Eucharist is a stumbling block for many — seemingly too mysterious, too miraculous, too divine, and so many do not accept Christ's presence in the Eucharist. The symbolic interpretation stems from the same early heresies that denied the truth of the Incarnation. Just as Christ was true man and true God, both fully present in both flesh and in spirit, he is now fully present in Body, Blood, Soul and Divinity in the Eucharist.

God sent His Son in the flesh to save us 2000 years ago, and still does today.

We must strengthen our catechesis in several areas ...

... not only to counter the arguments we hear from many by our separated brothers and sisters, on our belief in the Holy Eucharist – but Catholics too!

Here are some areas in catechesis that at times have been neglected. Though many videos and programs are available on these, they are often not fully covered or explained.

1. Better connections to the Old Testament (OT), especially the feast of Passover ... that the Mass and that the Eucharist are the fulfillment of the OT teachings. Just as they sacrificed a lamb and ate the lamb in a holy meal, Jesus brings this to completion and to perfection at the Last Supper. He is now the lamb to be sacrificed and eaten.

Use the example of Tent Sanctuary where the Jews had a table with the *bread of presence.* There is other imagery here that foreshadows the Mass.

Two Resources: Appendix Chapter 1: *The Jewish Roots of the Eucharist;*
Bibliography: *Jesus and the Dead Sea Scrolls*

2. New Testament. John chapter 6 is powerful. Jesus proclaims we must eat his flesh and drink His blood or we have no life of us. It is obvious, we must take it literally. Some Jews did not. At this, many of them left him.

It is important to realize that the eucharistic banquet is both a sacrifice *and* a meal. (CCC 1330,1383). Both are important. Today, there seems to be a deemphasis on the sacrificial aspects of the Mass. Remember: *there is no meal without the sacrifice, no table of the Lord without first the altar of the Lord!* Pope St. John Paul II mentions the sacrificial aspect in his encyclical (n.10):

At times one encounters an extremely reductive understanding of the Eucharistic mystery. Stripped of its sacrificial meaning, it is celebrated as if it were simply a fraternal banquet.

We must remember, for the sacrifice to be real, the victim must also be equally real, not *symbolically* present.

3. Church history. We need to demonstrate that this teaching was believed by all people in all places at all times up until the Protestant Reformation. We can draw from the earliest of the Christian writers and Church Fathers to prove this. And these quotes are available.[1] For example:

"... the food that has been made into the Eucharist ... is both the flesh and the blood of that incarnated Jesus." Justin Martyr 165 AD

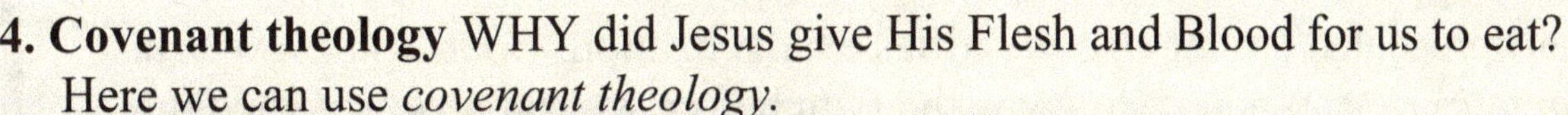

4. Covenant theology WHY did Jesus give His Flesh and Blood for us to eat? Here we can use *covenant theology.*

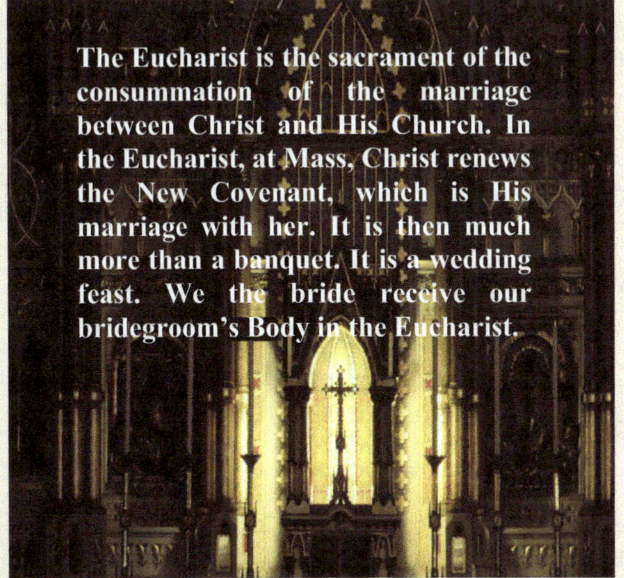

First, we cannot have a blood relationship with Jesus, so a covenant was established, which is a sacred familial bond. The Passover reestablishes the covenant with God. It was a sacred family bond (which still exists today). Every time the Jews celebrate this meal they are renewing this covenant with God.

Also, as the feast first originated (Exodus 12), the first born sons were marked for death and it was only through the sacrifice of the unblemished lamb and the *eating* of the lamb in a holy meal that they were saved.

Second, the covenant had to be renewed. Every time they ate this meal they renewed the covenant. The same is true for us. At Mass, through the Eucharist, we renew the covenant between Christ and His Church.

Remember that **Jesus came *not just to save us and redeem the world.* He came for us to have *union with God,*** that we might share in His divine life (2 Pt 1:4). St. Athanasius: *"For the Son of God became man so that we might become God."*

So it's not just accepting Jesus as our personal Lord and Savior ... to have Him come into our life. ***He invites us into His life*** *and that's why we have devotion to the Sacred Heart, and that's another reason why we receive the Holy Eucharist.*

5. Correct the errors. The Real Presence has sometimes been looked at as an obsolete form of eucharistic theology viewed instead as a communal presence of Christ in the gathered community. We need to correct those who believe that it's just symbolic, or that Jesus is "with" the Host, or "in" the Host that could be confusing. He's not *with* the Host. He IS the Host. This error is in some of our hymnals today. Have access to books on apologetics, such as Karl Keating's classic work, *Catholicism and Fundamentalism.*[2] This book is not just for Protestants, but also for Catholics.

And … we need to correct the error that once the Host is in small pieces it is no longer the Body and Blood of Jesus Christ, the influence of Karl Rahner's *Transcendental Thomism;*[3] or that we're not really holding Jesus, but merely the accidents, the color, the texture, etc. So any fragments on the floor are of no concern? It might be wise to review the CCC ns. 1374-77, and Appendix Chapter 4.

Evangelization

The pie chart presented earlier also identifies evangelization. *Good catechesis leads to good evangelization.* We have to *know* the faith before we can *proclaim* the faith and teach it to others. It could be your neighbor, friend, or a person sitting next to you in the pew who may need your help to understand their faith. A clue might be their irreverence, or a comment they make.

We should draw from techniques used in apologetics to teach or speak to others. It might be wise to review the basic skills related to apologetics as found in Chapter 14 of Karl Keating's work noted above. *How* to argue your point is as important as to *what* to argue. Style without substance is worthless; you must marry delivery with content. We need to go beyond *what* the Church teaches to *why* the Church teaches it. And remember, *being proceeds doing,* spending time in prayer and having recourse to sacraments with our dependence on God, not just relying on our own efforts.

Resources, Notes

1 William A. Jurgens, *The Faith of the Early Fathers,* (Collegeville, Minnesota: Liturgical Press, 1970); Volume 1 takes you through 382 AD with useful doctrinal index of Catholic teachings to locate written evidence of early belief.
2 Karl Keating, *Catholicism and Fundamentalism*, (San Francisco: Ignatius Press, 1988).
3. An attempt to reconcile the thought of Thomas Aquinas with the philosophy of Immanuel Kant.

DISCUSSION

As noted, we want better connections to the Old Testament.
For discussion on the foreshadowing of the Mass and the Eucharist in the Old Testament, see Appendix, Chapter 1 and the bibliography.

The Role of Catechesis to restore belief in the Real Presence

If we are going to employ catechesis to restore belief in the Real Presence, it might be useful to review Pope St John Paul II's 1979 Apostolic Exhortation *Catechesi Tradendae.* Here are a few of his key points that we can apply to our catechetical programs:

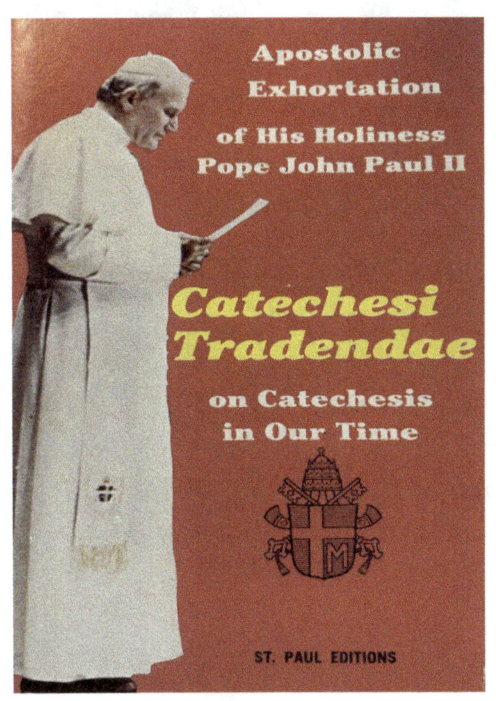

N. 7 *This teaching is not a body of abstract truths. It is the communication of the living mystery of God. The Person teaching it in the Gospel is altogether superior in excellence to the "masters" in Israel, and the nature of His doctrine surpasses theirs in every way because of the unique link between what He says, what He does and what He is. Nevertheless, the Gospels clearly relate occasions when Jesus "taught." "Jesus began to* ***do*** *and* ***teach****"* [emphasis added].

If we teach the faithful, especially the youth, about the Real Presence, then we must do what we teach. Do *we* ourselves exhibit the necessary reverence to support what we believe? Jesus "stirs up the people" with his teachings. We must stir up and inspire those we are teaching.

Ns. 12, 13 Do we apply the teachings of the Fathers and Doctors of the Church, those of the popes and saints: Paul VI, John Chysostom, Thomas Aquinas, Ambrose and Augustine?

Not only are their written works of great value and show the continuum and consistency of Church's teachings for 2000 years, but can inspire the faithful showing how they bore witness to this truth. Many suffered martyrdom and died defending or revering the Eucharist and a willingness to sacrifice for their beliefs. Who were they? What are their stories? … those who died attending Mass, those who died celebrating Mass, those who risked their lives protecting the Eucharist from desecration … St. Tarcisius, St Dominic Savio, and 11 year old Blessed Imelda Lambertini. ***They certainly believed in the Real Presence! No one is going to die for a symbol, a mere piece of bread.***

Our youth need to hear these stories of the martyrs of the Eucharist![4]

4 Great resource: Rev. J. Francis Sofie, OP, *Martyrs of the Eucharist:* Stories to Inspire Eucharistic Amazement, (Tan Books, Rockford, Ill., 2024).

Ns. 12, 13 Parents have a unique responsibility of fostering and teaching the faith to their children. This would include, of course, belief in the Real Presence.

One of the best ways to demonstrate our devotion is to regularly come before the Blessed Sacrament as a family with the children. *Do we do this?* We need to bear witness to what we believe.

St Theresa Parish, Trumbull, CT,

N. 23 Habits at an early age often carry-on to adulthood. It becomes a teaching moment.

" ... authentic practice of the sacraments is bound to have a catechetical aspect. In other words, sacramental life is impoverished and very soon turns into hollow ritualism if it is not based on serious knowledge of the meaning of the sacraments, and catechesis becomes intellectualized if it fails to come alive in the sacramental practice."

N. 54 Opportunities abound if one is observant. For example, locate exhibits on eucharistic miracles, participate in parish eucharistic processions and attend conferences at local parishes. Incorporate popular devotions into your family life.

N.73. Have recourse to Our Lady, Mother of the Holy Eucharist. Because Mary enfleshed Jesus, and since Jesus is the Eucharist, she also played a role in enfleshing the Eucharist. She is the Mother of the Blessed Sacrament. Love of the Eucharist and love of Our Lady must be central in the life of every Catholic Christian.

14th century Catholic theologian and mystic John Gerson wrote:
"You are the Mother of the Eucharist, because you are the Mother of Grace.
You more than all others after your Son, were aware of this Sacrament, hidden from the ages."

It's not enough to believe, we must act like we believe!

ACTION POINTS

It is important to remember that along with catechesis, prayer, fasting and sacrifices are an important response to the lack of belief in the Eucharist. Ultimately, it is the work of the Holy Spirit that brings conversion and faith, not merely our efforts and programs. Nevertheless, poor catechesis is an important element that has impacted the widespread disbelief in the Real Presence. So it's important to incorporate, prayer, fasting, etc. into our catechetical programs.

What ways can we improve our parish catechesis on the Eucharist?

… Invited Speakers?

… Parish bulletin articles?

… Expand the Adult Ed program (childcare for attending parents)

… Other:

Notes

Prayer by Fr. John Hardon

Mary, Mother of God, except for you, we would not have Jesus, and except for you, we would not have the Holy Eucharist, which is Jesus in our midst today.

Obtain for us a deep faith in the Blessed Sacrament. Help us to see the importance of the Eucharist in our Christian family, a community of life and love.

And that through the grace of the sacrament, our marriage bonds will be strengthened – Just as in the Eucharistic unity of Christ the bridegroom and his Bride, the Church, the expression of His "marriage" with humanity, grant that we may follow your example here on earth so that we might share in the joy that you experience in the visible company of your Son and Our Lord. Amen.

Chapter 2 Liturgical Music

Norms

The USCCB Specifically mentions liturgical music in PILLAR TWO ... promoting truth, goodness, and beauty.

The three *qualities* or characteristics which music *must* possess to be used in worship:

1) sanctity (principle point of reference)
2) goodness of form
3) universality of expression

Pope St. John Paul II:
" Sacred music" today has undergone such a broadening of meaning as to include repertoire that cannot enter into the celebration without violating the spirit and the norms of the Liturgy itself ... " (2004 Letter on 100th Anniversary of *Tra le Sollecitudini,* n. 4).

Pope Benedict XVI:
Sacred polyphony [1] *is a legacy that to be carefully preserved, kept alive, and propagated for the benefit ... of all the ecclesial community ...[and] cannot be achieved except by following the great traditions of the past ...* (at 2006 concert of sacred music, Sistine Chapel).

Pope Francis:
A certain mediocrity, superficiality, and banality have prevailed to the detriment of the beauty and intensity of the liturgical celebrations ... (2017 Conference on Sacred Music).

The seldom read governing document is Pius X's *Tra le Sollecitudini* (TLS) issued moto proprio cited in Vatican II documents (*Musicam Sacram,* n.4, fn. 2).[2]

Pope St. John Paul II in his 2004 Letter:
It is indeed important that the musical compositions utilized in liturgical celebrations conform to the criteria opportunely pronounced by St. Pius X and wisely developed both by the 2nd Vatican Council and by the successive authoritative teaching of the Church.

Pius X issuing TLS
Cathedral of the Assumption
Covington, Kentucky

TWO Goals of Church worship: *giving glory to God AND sanctifying and edifying Christian souls.* Sacred music is *indispensable to Christian worship.* Specific causes of the problems cited by the three pontiffs are addressed in TLS that still apply today are ...

1) the rapid changeability of tastes and habits
2) the bad influence of secular and theatrical style
3) music for music's sake
4) the tendency toward deviating from right rules and purposes when it comes to selecting music for worship

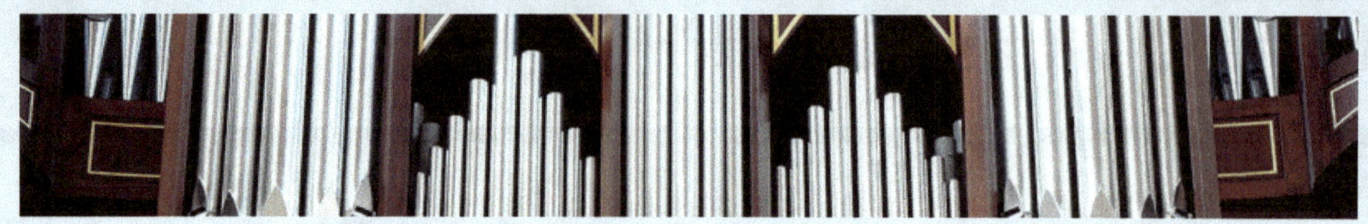

So why is all this important in the Eucharistic Revival?

Today's "approved" hymnals need to be critiqued for theological accuracy. Many hymns at best trivialize or mislead us on the truths of the faith, especially the Eucharist. These hymns have no business in our liturgy.

Many of the hymns at Mass, especially during the distribution of the Eucharist, deemphasize or ignore the Real Presence. Some have nothing to do with the Eucharist. Many of the traditional hymns that do emphasize the Real Presence of God have "gone the way of the dinosaurs."

Some hymns are heretical stating that Jesus is present with the sacred Host. He is not with the Host (consubstantiation). He is the Host.

Actual case: A parishioner brought up to the parochial vicar a hymn with this issue and his response was: "Oh, only you would recognize that." If this person is the only one recognizing that, then this affirms the poor catechesis they have at that parish on transubstantiation. Everyone should've recognized that! Also …

The meal or table aspect is emphasized over the altar. "Altar" denotes sacrifice. Replacing "altar" with "table" in our lyrics ignores the sacrificial aspect of the Mass. There are cases where the words have blatantly been changed, as in the well known hymn *Praise to the Lord.* This example is brought to light in the Discussion to follow.

Some contemporary hymns lead us to believe that Christ becomes bread, or the Eucharist is just a symbol rather than Christ Himself, or often overemphasizing the meal aspect or some social justice action. See Discussion fn. 3 for examples.

Therefore, regarding liturgical music, in this time of eucharistic revival and for the sake of our discussion here, we must be alert to our selected hymns that may not be theologically sound. Let us instead promote those that do emphasize the Real Presence to reinforce what our belief is in this regard. .

Resources, Notes

1 Sacred polyphony: Two or more independent melodies interwoven to create harmony.

2 Review the Second Vatican Council Conciliar and Post Conciliar documents pertaining to Sacred music: The Constitution on the Sacred Liturgy *Sacrosanctum Consilium*, ns 112-122, and: *Musicam Sacram* 1967 Instruction on Music in the Liturgy.: https://www.vatican.va/archive/hist_councils/ii_vatican_council/documents/vat-ii_instr_19670305_musicam-sacram_en.html. and for TLS (*Tra le Sollecitudini):* https://www.papalencyclicals.net/pius10/tra-le-sollecitudini.htm. Both Accessed August 7, 2025.

Discussion

Regarding word changes to our hymns:
Example. The sacrificial aspects of the Mass.

There is no table of the Lord without first the <u>altar</u> of the Lord.

Pope St. John Paul II. *Ecclesia de Eucharistia*, n. 10:
At times one encounters an extremely reductive understanding of the Eucharistic mystery. Stripped of its sacrificial meaning, it is celebrated as if it were simply a fraternal banquet.

Example:
***Gather* Second and Third Editions**
GIA Publications
Still in use in some parishes.

2nd Edition:
... "Praise to the Lord" (#536)

Original Hymn lyrics:
Now to His *<u>altar</u>* draw near ...
Changed to:

Now to the *temple* draw near,
Or:
Brothers and sisters draw near ...

Be alert for hymns that degrade the Eucharist in any manner, s suggesting for example, that Jesus is *in* the Host. or *with* the Host ... or hymns that deny the sacrificial aspect of the Mass.

Bring these to the attention first to your faith formation lead who can check the theology, then your music director, your pastor, and, if necessary, your office of worship in your diocese. Bottom line: We need more hymns that emphasize the Real Presence.

---

3 Besides over emphasizing the table or a meal aspect, just a few examples of hymns that can confuse us with regard to our Lord as merely bread and wine, in the bread or in the wine, or just a symbol.
Just a symbol: *Bless the Feast,* James Hansen 1988 OCP; Jesus in the bread and wine: *Supper of the Lord* Lawrence Rosania 1994 OCP, *In Remembrance of You,* Paul A Tate 1997 WLP; Emphasis on Table or Meal: *Table of Plenty* Dan Schutte 1992. OCP.

Use of Traditional Hymns

Make an effort with your music director to select hymns that promote the Real Presence of Jesus in the Eucharist. Yes, they might be pre-Vatican II. So what? What do the Vatican II documents say? It's an indisputable fact that the second Vatican did not intend to do away with traditional hymns including Gregorian chant:

The musical tradition of the universal Church is a treasure of inestimable value, greater even than that of any other art. The main reason for this pre-eminence is that, as sacred song is united to the words, it forms a necessary or integral part of the solemn liturgy … The treasure of sacred music is to be <u>preserved and fostered</u> with great care. *Sacrosanctum Concilium,* ns. 112, 114.

Sadly, we have been so inundated with contemporary music, many Catholics have forgotten the words to many of these priceless eucharistic or communion hymns, many of them sung during 40 hours devotions (see Chapter Four). What happened to the hymns such as:

Lord Jesus I adore thee, Soul of my Savior, O Sanctissima, O Lord I am not Worthy, Oh Jesus, we adore thee, At the first Eucharist ...

How many remember this communion hymn ... *Jesus Thou Art Coming?*

> *Jesus thou Art coming, holy as thou art, thou, the God who made me, to my sinful heart. Jesus, I believe it on the only Word, kneeling, I adore thee, as my King and Lord.*

Parishioners or choir directors who express an interest in traditional music are sometimes told: *"It is inappropriate for the post-Vatican II Church."*

In response, to label a hymn as outdated given the magnificent history of liturgical music in the Church is nothing more than being a slave of the moment. See three hymnal options in Action Points.

In summary, while the Council encouraged participation by the people of God so *"the voices of the faithful may ring out"* (n. 118) ... they urged that the treasure of sacred music be preserved as noted above.

Comment from an editorial:

A great majority of today's eucharistic hymns refer to "sharing bread and wine" ... A hymn is simply prayer set to music... As we pray so too we believe ... many Catholics who attend Sunday Mass are exposed to this eucharistic heresy. We should be singing about receiving Christ's Body and Blood ... Either the liturgical musicians and publishing companies are ignorant of this ... or they do know what the Church teaches about the Holy Eucharist but are attempting to change this belief by making the congregation sing hymns that do not reflect authentic Catholic teaching ... in my estimation, this is a grave problem that needs immediate attention.

Musicam Sacram

This key 1967 document following Vatican II was issued to clarify some points and to dispel any confusion and preserve the Church's treasury of sacred music encouraging Gregorian chants and music taken from traditional heritage:

MUSICAM SACRAM
ET LITURGIAM AUTHENTICAM

***Musicians will enter on this new work with the desire to continue that tradition which has furnished the Church, in her divine worship, with truly an abundant heritage.* n. 59**

Cardinal Arinze, prior Prefect of Divine Worship and the Discipline of the Sacraments notes, much of our music is often *"... poor in theological content, not firmly rooted in Tradition, have little or no scriptural overtones and do not build up the faith of those that sing or listen to them* [composed by] *individuals just composing anything, and singing it in Church ..."*

Liturgical music at Mass must be suited to the sacred action. Remember that all the gestures, prayers, antiphons, etc., reveal our belief in the Real Presence and orient us toward the re-presentation of the Sacrifice of Calvary and ultimately the reception of Holy Communion by the faithful.

Should we not teach, especially our youth, the glory of our rich patrimony? Should we not expose them to the great Catholic composers and artists that have gone before us? This teaches us that the faith of the Church, including what we believe about the Eucharist, has been intertwined in all of our sacred music since our very beginnings. As we pray so too we believe. As we sing so to we believe.

ACTION POINTS

What ways can I encourage more hymns that reinforce our belief in the Real Presence?

What Hymnals have traditional hymns? Some options:

Adoremus Hymnal **by Ingnatius Press**

Also by Ignatius Press: ***Pew Missal*** **with the Sunday Readings**

Credo Hymnal **which is a complete traditional hymnal that includes not only a wide selection of chant and well-known traditional hymns and songs, but also new titles from Catholic composers that specialize in traditional music (office@ilpmusic.org OR call 615-599-4497).**

There are others.

Notes:

Prayers to Saint Cecilia

Eternal God, you gave us the gift of St. Cecilia, a powerful protector and patron of music. We strive to pass our days faithfully and innocently like holy St. Cecilia so that we may come to Heaven where we may praise you in concert with her. Amen

O glorious St. Cecilia, virgin and martyr, you won the martyr's crown without renouncing your love for Jesus, the delight of your soul. We ask that you help us to be faithful in our love for Jesus, that, in the communion of the saints, we may praise Him twice in our song of rejoicing for the Blood that He shed which gave us the grace to accomplish His will on earth. Amen.

O glorious Saint, who chose to die instead of denying your King. We pray you please to help us as His fair praise we sing! We lift our hearts in joyous song to honor Him this way. And while we sing, remembering to sing is to doubly pray. At once in our hearts and our tongues we offer double prayer sent heavenward on winged notes to praise God dwelling there. While with our hearts and tongues we try with song to praise God twice. We ask dear Saint to help us be united close with Christ! Amen.

Chapter 3 Dress Code And Decorum

Dress Code

This is a hot button topic ... often afraid to address.

Few dress in any special way for Church these days. In most parishes "extreme casual" would seem to be the norm of the day. Most people don't even think to change their clothes for church; there is a "go as you are" mentality. [1]

Does our dress for Mass reflect in any way respect for what we are about to receive who is present in our church, and our willingness to be presentable to our God in a special way?

Is there a dress code for attending Mass?

Are there any norms for modest dress?

The answer is, "Yes, in accord with the virtue of modesty."

In his Letter to the Galatians, St. Paul lists modesty as one of the fruits of the Holy Spirit, those "perfections that the Holy Spirit forms in us as the first fruits of eternal glory" (Galatians 5:22-23; CCC, n. 1832.).

As a youth, this author had special clothes he would wear to Mass. Why? Church was a special place. Mass was a sacred occasion. Here he would be receiving his Lord Jesus Christ.

By the virtue of modesty, the devout person governs all his exterior acts. With good reason, then, does Saint Paul recommend this virtue to all and declare how necessary it is and as if this were not enough he considers that this virtue should be obvious to all.

Pio of Pietrelcina

The virtue of

MODESTY

If I do not become a saint, I am doing nothing.

Saint Dominic Savio

Father John Hardon, S.J. defined modesty as follows:

The virtue that moderates all the internal and external movements and appearance of a person according to his or her endowments, possessions, and station of life. Four virtues are commonly included under modesty: humility, studiousness, and two kinds of external modesty, namely in dress and general behavior. (The Pocket Catholic Dictionary, 1985).

The *Catechism of the Catholic Church* expounds upon these principles:

Modesty protects the intimate center of the person. It means refusing to unveil what should remain hidden. It is ordered to chastity to whose sensitivity it bears witness. It guides how one looks at others and behaves toward them in conformity with the dignity of person and their solidarity. Modesty protects the mystery of persons and their love. It encourages patience and moderation in loving relationships; it requires that the conditions for the definitive giving and commitment of man and woman to one another be fulfilled. Modesty is decency. It inspires one's choice of clothing. It keeps silence or reserve where there is evident risk of unhealthy curiosity. It is discreet (ns. 2521, 2522).

The Catholic needs to ask …
What am I stating by what I am wearing?
In other words: what is the "packaging," what is the advertising?
What am I trying to draw attention to?

If the intent is to show off the body and to arouse the sexual feelings of another, or to draw attention to oneself and pique the curiosity of another, then one has violated modesty in dress and behavior.

A parishioner brought this to the attention of the parents of a young lady at Mass, who brought the gifts to the altar, in inappropriate attire. Her dress was halfway up her thighs. The parent's response? "Well, it's the style."

Similarly, some may respond, "That is not my intention. These are today's fashions. I should not be judged by my clothes." Yet, often people are judged by their clothes. Why else do people try to look their best for a job interview or meeting a head of state? Why else do most companies have dress codes?

The reality is …
clothes send a certain message and reveal the spiritual disposition of the person.

There is another account of a young lady at Mass wearing a dress exposing six inches of her waist, the front cut very low, and her shoulders bare.
Someone said to her very discreetly: "Please dress appropriately for Mass."

Her father later approached him, yelled at him, and physically threatened him. Instead of guiding and guarding their daughter, he and his wife adopted a permissive attitude which endangers body and soul.

And it's not just women …men too, sometimes in gym shorts and T shirts. There are cases of young men or boys at Mass wearing T-shirts with skulls and crossbones, almost satanic in its presentation.

We encounter other denominations, for example, the Baptists, having Sunday lunch after attending their services, all dressed up "to the hilt." How much more so should we dress up given who is present in our churches at the Catholic Mass?

Is there is a dress code?

Of course, everyone is invited to Mass, but there are certain expectations when you come. Just like when you go to a synagogue, as a man, you are invited to wear a yamaka on your head … because this is *their* home.
You are in their holy space.

There IS a dress code to enter a Catholic church.
This is our home.
This is our holy space.

Is there a standard?

The Catechism of the Catholic Church speaks about dressing properly. "Bodily demeanor (gestures, clothing) ought to convey the respect, solemnity, and joy of this moment when Christ becomes our guest" (CCC 1387). St. Peters Basilica in Rome has a dress code that must be followed by all visitors, irrespective of age or gender. Like St. Peters, some parishes do have a picture or a decal, reflecting this dress code … what you can wear and what you cannot wear. And if you do not comply with this dress code, you may be asked to not enter.
Come dressed in proper attire.

All are welcome. But there are standards. [3]

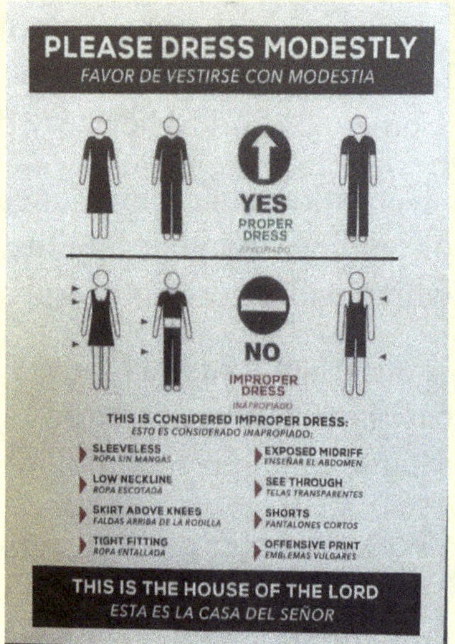

So why aren't we talking about it?
Are we dressing appropriately given
the Real Presence of Jesus Christ in this sacred place?

If we were going to a job interview, visiting the monarch of the UK, or attending an opera on a Saturday night, how would we dress for that? How much more important is the Mass and who we are coming before?

Of course, if we don't believe in the Real Presence, then, why bother … nothing going on in here that's very special.

Dressing appropriately is one more practice that needs to be restored because not enforcing it is eroding our belief in the Real Presence. If God is NOT in there, if His Real Presence is not in there, why should I dress special for the Mass? Then, no big deal, right?

All of these bad practices add up and erode our belief, especially those who may be present who don't believe. If I don't dress like I believe in the Real Presence, in time I may not believe anymore.
In the end, dress code is not about rules. It's about love of Jesus.

Resources, Notes

1 From article by Monsignor Charles Pope in the NCR. See Discussion page 51.
2 Vatican Dress Code: https://www.st-peters-basilica-tickets.com/st-peters-basilica-dress-code/. Accessed October 1, 2023.
3 **See Appendix Chapter Three** (Most Rev. Thomas John Paprocki Bishop, Diocese of Springfield).

Decorum

Respect for the Lord's True Presence …

On entering the Church we are expected to maintain a *sacred silence.* We should bless ourselves with holy water and, to be discussed later, some gesture of reverence directed toward the tabernacle, and genuflect upon entering a pew.

Silent prayer is expected prior to Mass, to prepare ourselves, for the proper disposition for why we are there.

And, also, it is recommended to at least spend a few minutes in thanksgiving after Mass. Few do.

Someone could be praying

Some Catholics do remain after Mass to pray amid the noise and commotion that typically follows most of our Masses. If not for the Lord's True Presence, then at least out of *courtesy* to others, silence should be maintained, holding off conversations until outside the main church and sanctuary.

Besides out of courtesy, we should remain in silence as best as possible in the pew. Get to church early enough for time to pray, review the readings, etc. See Discussion.

Often, there is considerable noise already. Some Catholics come and go like they're attending a sporting event. Maybe it's the chatter at the entrance with the hospitality greeters, or someone twanging on a guitar in the choir.

In some parishes to maintain decorum, a Rosary or Divine Mercy is prayed prior to Mass. Now there's an idea!! In another parish: the priest reminds everyone to depart in silence, or ends with the St. Michael Prayer, *Salve Regina* and a prayer for vocations.

If we wish to have fellowship and discussion, then let it follow after Mass outside the church proper. One approach, if someone wishes to talk to you, is to kindly ask to hold off until we are outside, perhaps in the hall or narthex. Priests can help by reminding people to hold down the chatter.

Unnecessary noise, commotion, etc. is disrespectful to our Lord, who is present Body, Blood, Soul, and Divinity in this sacred place.

As already noted in the RPC survey, lack of decorum and silence has over the years eroded belief in the Real Presence.

DISCUSSION

Promoting a Sacred Silence

It's not enough to believe, we must act like we believe!

As Msgr. Pope suggested (Chapter 5), the issue of how we enter the church is tied to one of the major issues facing the Church today substantiated statistically in many surveys: ***the loss of belief in the Real Presence of Jesus Christ in the Holy Eucharist is in turn closely tied to the loss in the sense of the sacred.***

Cardinal Robert Sarah: [1] "... a person can recollect himself, but if he is not capable of holding his tongue, his meditation will not help him to enter into the mystery of God or to prostrate himself silently at the foot of his throne ... Where kneeling and genuflection have disappeared from the liturgy, they need to be restored, in particular for our reception of the blessed Lord in Holy Communion". ***Christians enter a church for the liturgical celebration, how many acknowledge Christ's presence in the tabernacle and honor him with a genuflection accompanied by a moment of prayer?***

It is important that we do not contribute to the noise and conversations that may be present before and after Mass. It is difficult when people approach you and begin to converse, even if it is a relatively important matter. We must try to encourage them to join you in conversation outside the main sanctuary. **Observe the "5 R's "...**

- **REVERENCE:**
  It creates a sacred atmosphere, emphasizing the Real Presence of God.
- **REMEMBER**
  Silence helps to clear the mind and remember the purpose of attending Mass, leading to a more meaningful experience. It provides a space for us to recall past blessings, reflect on God's generosity, and prepare their hearts for encountering the Lord.
- **READINGS:**
  Provides quiet time to review the readings. How is the Old and New Testament connected? How do these readings apply to what might be going on in my own life? If you were giving the homily, how would you present it?
- **RAISING our minds and hearts to God in Prayer:**
  It allows individuals to offer their personal intentions and prayers, both for themselves and others, before the Mass begins.
- **RESPECT**
  It demonstrates respect for the sacred space and courtesy for those who are also seeking a quiet moment of prayer.

While some quiet conversation is unavoidable, especially when we have children, the emphasis should be on creating a space conducive to prayer and reflection. The goal is to transition from the everyday noisy world into a more focused and prayerful mindset as the Mass begins.

Observing the 5 R's!

The *General Instruction for the Roman Missal* (GIRM, no. 45) says that there should be a quiet opportunity in the church for the faithful to prepare prayerfully for the Holy Mass.

St Faustina's diary [2] ... on silence, which applies especially before Mass:

Entry 118: In order to hear the voice of God, one has to have silence in one's soul and to keep silence; not a gloomy silence but an interior silence; that is to say, recollected in God.

Entry 552:
The Holy Spirit does not speak to a soul that is distracted and garrulous (talkative). He speaks by His quiet inspirations to a soul that is recollected, to a soul that knows how to keep silence.

Entry 1008:
The Lord gave me to know how displeased He is with a talkative soul. I find no rest in such a soul. The constant din tires Me, and in the midst of it the soul cannot discern My voice.

Entry 477: Silence is a sword in the spiritual struggle. A talkative soul will never attain sanctity. The sword of silence will cut off everything that would like to cling to the soul ...

... *Without silence, there is no reverence,* there is no recollection, no contemplation, no communication with Our LORD, and no spiritual life.

Those who do not keep silent not only cause great harm to themselves; they are a cause of *distraction for others* and do not allow them to pray and talk to the LORD as they would like to.

Author Charles Belmonte encourages us to also pray on the way to Mass:

Prepare your soul for Communion with acts of love of God. Make acts of contrition and atonement...pray for the priest that he may truly minister to the needs of the parish. Pray for the congregation...pray that you may understand what you yourself will be taught at Mass ("Understanding the Mass," p. 38*).*

Silence should also be observed after Mass until one is outside the Church building, both for respect toward the Blessed Sacrament, and toward those members of the faithful who wish to prolong their thanksgiving after Mass.

As we enter the church, be it for Mass or other activity, remember, we are coming into the presence of God. This is <u>holy</u> ground.

Robert Cardinal Sarah's work *The Power of Silence* is worthy of review. [3]

Sacred silence also, as part of the celebration, is to be observed at the designated times ... as the GIRM says: *Its purpose, however, depends on the time it occurs in each part of the celebration. Thus within the Act of Penitence and again after the invitation to pray, all recollect themselves; but at the conclusion of a reading or the homily, all meditate briefly on what they have heard; then after Communion, they praise and pray to God in their hearts and pray to him..*

Even before the celebration itself, it is commendable that silence [to] be observed in the church, *in the sacristy, in the vesting room, and in adjacent areas, so that all may dispose themselves to carry out the sacred action in a devout and fitting manner.*

There is ... a time to keep silence and time to speak (Eccles 3:7) ***...***
he should keep silent when it is not necessary to speak, and he should speak when necessity or charity requires it.

Cardinal Sarah speaks of the *dictatorship of noise* present in our society.

We live in a noisy society ... do we bring that in with us when we arrive at church?

A noisy society is like sorry, looking cardboard, stage scenery, a world without substance, an immature flight. A noisy church would become vain, unfaithful, and dangerous.

Entering the church, we are entering sacred ground with the presence of God ...

We must learn to keep silence and to nourish it with the presence of God ...

Silence teaches us a great rule of the spiritual life: familiarity does not promote intimacy; on the contrary a proper distance is a condition for communion. Humanity advances toward love through adoration, Sacred silence, laden with the adored presence, opens the way to mystical silence, full of loving intimacy. Under the yolk of secular reason, which only makes us feel guilty, we have forgotten that worship and the sacred are the only entrances to the spiritual life.

And ...

Sacred silence, offers us a way of leaving the profane world and the incessant turmoil of our immense metropolitan cities so as to allow God to take hold of us. Sacred silence is truly the place where we can encounter God, because we come to him with the proper attitude of a man who trembles and stands at a distance while hoping confidently. Sacred silence is therefore the only truly human and Christian reaction to God when he breaks into our lives.

So what do you do, especially upon leaving, when someone wants to chat?

Pope Francis (*National Catholic Register,* Nov. 15, 2017):

When we go to Mass, maybe we arrive five minutes before, and we start to chitchat with those in front of us ... However, it is not a moment for chitchat.

It is a moment of silence for preparing ourselves for dialogue, a time for the heart to collect itself in order to prepare for the encounter with Jesus, he said, *adding that* ***silence is so important.***

You want to take your conversations outside. If someone starts chatting with you, encourage the person to quietly join you in the narthex or outside.

---

1 https://www.thescottsmithblog.com/2020/03/the-essential-quotes-of-robert-cardinal.html. Accessed July 8, 2025.

2 Excellent Resource: "The Fate of Talkative Souls, the Value of Silence," https://www.thedivinemercy.org/articles/fate-talkative-souls-value-silence. Accessed July 1, 2025.

3 Robert Cardinal, Sarah, *The Power of Silence* (San Francisco: Ignatius Press, 2017) pp. 121, 122, 137, 239, 240.

Te Deum

You are God: we praise you;
you are the Lord we acclaim you;
you are the eternal Father:
All creation worships you.

To you all angels, all the powers of heaven
Cherubim and Seraphim, sing in endless praise:
Holy, holy, holy, Lord, God of power and might,
Heaven and earth are full of your glory.

The glorious company of the Apostles: praise you.
The goodly fellowship of the Prophets: praise you.
The noble army of martyrs: praise you.

Throughout the world
The Holy Church acclaims you:
Father, of majesty unbounded,
Your true and only Son, worthy of all worship,
And the Holy Spirit, advocate and guide.

You, Christ, are the King of Glory,
The eternal Son of the Father.
When you became man to set us free
You did not spurn the Virgin's womb.

You overcame the sting of death,
And opened the Kingdom of Heaven to all believers.
You are seated at God's right hand and glory.
We believe that you will come, and be our judge.

Come then, Lord, and help your people,
bought with the price of your blood,
And bring us with your saints
To glory everlasting. Amen.

ACTION POINTS

Catechists need to talk about some of these points …

What behaviors in society have brought about noise in sacred places?

What aspect of our culture enables irreverence to God in the church and before the Blessed Sacrament?

What polite ways can we bring to the attention of others to wear proper attire for Mass? How can we encourage our pastor to ask people to dress appropriately? There is always a fear of losing parishioners.

Perhaps encourage your pastor to install decals on your front doors as some parishes have done. A parish in Louisiana placed the dress code standards on a plastic card for all the pews.

How can we encourage others near us to remain quiet before and after Mass?

Can you have sacred music such as chant playing in church before Mass?

How can we encourage our pastor to be involved in all of the above?

Notes

An Act of Faith in the Real Presence

Lord Jesus Christ, I believe you are as truly present in this Holy Sacrament, under the signs of bread and wine, as you were when dying upon a cross for the salvation of all mankind, or as you are now enthroned in glory in heaven at the right hand of the Father. You said that you would give us yourself as the Bread of Life, which, if we eat, we shall live forever. I believe this truth because you are truth itself. With confidence in your loving forgiveness, therefore, I approach your altar, conscious that my unworthiness to receive you is outweighed by your desire to be united with my soul. You desire to nourish it on its earthly pilgrimage, until the day when I shall be with you in the eternal banquet, to feed on the unveiled beauty of your presence forever. **Amen.**

Chapter 4 Adoration

The USCCB document makes a strong push for Adoration / Exposition of the Blessed Sacrament. [1] ***This must be an important part of our Revival. Sadly, attendance and opportunities for Adoration are lacking in many parishes.***

Real Presence demands real attention!

Excuses:

<u>ARGUMENT 1</u>: "Well, He is there in the tabernacle already."

From a catechetical standpoint, many do not know the distinction between our Lord's presence in the tabernacle and Exposition of the Blessed Sacrament. They are not exactly the same. We need to make that distinction.

Eucharistic Exposition is the ritual by which it is displayed outside the tabernacle in a monstrance for <u>public</u> veneration by the faithful.

It is a public celebration that enables the faithful to perceive more clearly the relationship between the reserved sacrament, and the sacrifice of the Mass and the purpose of the worship of Eucharist outside Mass.

A wonderful image of our Lord given to us by Saint Faustina ... the rays streaming out from the Heart of Jesus as she describes in her work and her writings.

There are 3 purposes and added benefits of exposition of the Blessed Sacrament:

1) Leads us to a full participation in the celebration of the Eucharist, culminating in Holy Communion;

2) Fosters worship, which is due Christ in spirit and in truth;

3) The fruits, which include vocations!

There have been numerous examples cited in the Catholic press [2] that in parishes that have Perpetual Adoration, or extended hours of adoration, vocations increase. Want more vocations? Provide more time for Adoration of the Blessed Sacrament!

In addition:

We must explain that our Lord is not adored any less because it was instituted by Christ to be eaten. He is substantially there, and is reserved to *extend the grace of the sacrifice.*

ARGUMENT 2: ... Not enough time or space.
Well, there is no room for this here.
We have so many parish ministries.
There's no space. No days and times to work it in.
Besides, another parish nearby has it. Go there.

Reminds us of Mary and Joseph desperately searching for a place to give birth to Jesus; there's no room in the inn (Lk 2:7). Through Adoration, we give a rebirth of Christ in our parish ... in the world!

There is the true story of a new parish pastor now in a large parish with over 50 ministries. He canceled most of them to focus on the most important. At the top of his list was time before the Blessed Sacrament. Where are our priorities today? We should not have to go elsewhere.

There is a small church in Lee, Massachusetts, Mary Mother of the Church parish. They don't have large parish facilities with thousands of square feet. But they found room for our Lord. In the back, they built a small structure specifically for Perpetual Adoration.

Mary Mother of the Church parish, Lee, MA.

ARGUMENT 3: "No One will Come ..."
Start! ... THEN people will come!
Provide homilies and prep to organize and begin Adoration. Again, you should not have to travel to another parish to have time before the Blessed Sacrament.

Pope St. John Paul II (1980 Letter to the Episcopal Conference of Germany):

The Church and the World have a great need of Eucharistic Worship. Jesus waits for us in the sacrament of love, let us be generous in our time in going to meet him in adoration and in contemplation that is full of faith, and ready to make reparation for the great faults and crimes of the world.
May our adoration never cease.

Mother Teresa:

The time you spend with Jesus in the Blessed Sacrament will be the best, the most profitable time you will ever spend here on earth!

PERPETUAL EUCHARISTIC
Adoration

The best time you will spend on earth is the time that you spend with your Best Friend, Jesus, in the Blessed Sacrament."
– Mother Teresa of Calcutta

How can we enter the church, regardless of the reasons we are there, and not at least make a five minute visit to the tabernacle?

Activism seems to abound.
Everyone is busy doing things.
But how many spend time before the Blessed Sacrament?

Perpetual Adoration …

Besides more time weekly for Exposition, and as the USCCB stressed, we too need to work more toward having Perpetual Adoration in ALL our parishes.

St. Mother Teresa, ardent supporter of Perpetual Adoration:

When you look at the crucifix you understand how much Jesus loves you. When you look at the sacred Host, you understand how much Jesus loves you now! This is why you should ask your parish priest to have Perpetual Adoration at your parish. I beg the Blessed Mother to touch the hearts of all parish priests that they may have Perpetual Adoration in their parishes and that it will spread throughout the whole world.

If Jesus stays with us wherever there is a consecrated Host, what need is there to go on pilgrimage to Jerusalem to visit places he lived two thousand years ago? If only people visited tabernacles with the same devotion! – St. Carlo Acutis

As the USCCB also recommended, we need to revive our 40 hours devotion that seems to have faded over the years. See Discussion.

Resources, Notes

1 As in Pillar One and Five (see Introduction), also: *Thirty-One questions on Adoration of the Blessed Sacrament*, Bishop Committee on the Liturgy, USCCB, Washington DC, 2005.

2 Examples: "Eucharistic Devotion Serves as Catalyst for Young Men Discerning Priesthood," https://www.ncregister.com/features/eucharistic-devotion-serves-as-catalyst-for-young-men-discerning-priesthood, (accessed 7-8-25): "Perpetual Adoration and Vocations," https://vocationblog.com/2014/09/perpetual-adoration-and-vocations/. Accessed July 8, 2025.

3 Additional Resources:

Vatican Council II, *Sacrosanctum Concilium,* Chapter 3, *Eucharisticum Mysterium*, Instruction on the Worship of the Eucharistic Mystery, ns 58-67.

Pope St. John Paul II, *Ecclesia de Eucharistia.* 2003, Especially ns. 10 and 25.

Pope St .John Paul II, *Dominicae Cenae,* On the Mystery of the Eucharist, n.3.

DISCUSSION

Renewing the 40 Hours Devotion

Come and spend time with our Eucharistic King!

The 40 hours devotion is the practice that involves continuous prayer for forty hours before the Blessed Sacrament exposed. The Devotion is also called "Quarant'Ore" or written in one word *Quarantore.*

The precise origin of the Forty Hours Devotion is not clear. The Milanese chronicler Burigozzo describes the custom of exposing the Blessed Sacrament in one church after another as a novelty which began at Milan in 1537. Two years later we have the reply of Pope Paul III to a petition soliciting indulgences for the practice. St. Charles Borromeo promoted this ancient practice. It consists of praying before the Blessed Sacrament exposed for forty hours; and he compares it to the 40 hours that Christ's Body remained in the tomb. The number 40 appears often associated with biblical events. It is an excellent way for a parish to expand our eucharistic devotions during this period of renewal. Key aspects and prayers of the Forty Hours Devotion can be found on line and in devotional booklets.[4]

- **Continuous Prayer:**

  The core of the devotion is the continuous prayer and hymns offered before the Blessed Sacrament for 40 hours.

- **Blessed Sacrament Exposition:**

  The Eucharist solemnly exposed in a monstrance on the altar for all to adore.

- **Community Gathering:**

  It's a time for the community to come together and pray before the Blessed Sacrament, fostering a sense of unity. The Eucharist is the "sacrament of unity."

- **Purpose:**

  The aim is to deepen the faithful's love for the Eucharist, foster a deeper relationship with Christ, and seek His blessings for themselves, their community, and the world.

- **Activities:**

  The devotion may include solemn Masses, hymns, eucharistic processions, periods of silent prayer, and reflections on the Eucharist.

  The current practice has seen a renewal, especially since the USCCB three year Revival. It is an important practice that focuses on the Real Presence and should be implemented by all parishes at least once a year.

4 For example: https://www.saintmaryswashingtonville.com/documents/2022/2/40%20Hours%20Prayer%20Booklet%20St MarysWash-1.pdf. Accessed August 6, 2025.

ACTION POINTS

Following St. Mother Teresa's advice, how do we encourage our parish priest to move toward perpetual adoration?

Examples:
Start small, more times for adoration weekly.
Increase as more adorers sign up.
Programs and speakers to inspire the faithful.

Many dioceses began the practice of Perpetual Adoration by the 1970s. The practice still survives in many parishes to this day. While many of the laity are dedicated toward encouraging and assisting in days of parish eucharistic adoration, the parish priest is of utmost importance. The faithful will always follow a good shepherd.

It would be good to know the rules and format for the 40 hours devotion so you can present it to your pastor with a *plan in mind,* rather than to just suggest it. Have examples of the materials ready to order for your pastor to review (for example, the booklet noted on page 44 fn) and a list of the parishioners and parish ministries who will help.

Notes

Prayer of St. Francis

Let everyone be struck with fear,
let the whole world tremble,
and let the heavens exult
when Christ,
the Son of the living God,
is present on the altar
in the hands of a priest!

O wonderful loftiness
and stupendous dignity!
O sublime humility!
O humble sublimity!

The Lord of the universe, God and the Son of God,
so humbles Himself that for our salvation He hides Himself
under an ordinary piece of bread!

Brothers, look at the humility of God,
and pour out your hearts before Him!
Humble yourselves
that you may be exalted by Him!

Hold back nothing of yourselves for yourselves,
that He Who gives Himself totally to you
may receive you totally!

Prayer of Fr. Lawrence Lovasik [5]

Eternal praise and thanks to You, Jesus Christ,
Son of God, made man,
born of the Blessed Virgin, for the mercy and love You have shown
to Holy Mother Church,
and to me in particular, in this sacrament.

I unite my voice of praise and my sentiments of love
with those of the angels and saints in Heaven,
with Mary -- their Queen,
and Our Lady of the Most Blessed Sacrament –
and with all Your faithful children on earth.

I thank You, divine Word, Incarnate,
for the Real Presence of Your Body and Blood, Soul, and divinity
among us under the veils of bread and wine;
for Your Sacrifice of Calvary,
renewed in an unbloody manner our altars at holy Mass,
at which we offer You to God as a Victim, worthy of His Majesty
and as a Gift that fulfills all our obligations to Him;
for the supreme privilege of receiving You as the Bread of Life
and of being united so closely to You in Holy Communion.

May my whole life be an unending
hymn of praise and thanksgiving to You
for this most wonderful Gift: the Eucharist!

O Sacrament most holy, O Sacrament, divine,
all praise and all thanksgiving, be every moment thine!

Lawrence G. Lovasik (1913 - 1986)

Ordained in 1938, Fr. Lovasik was a member of the missionary Society of the Divine Word. He was born of Slovak parents in the steel town of Tarentum Pennsylvania. He went on to do missionary work in America's coal and steel regions. In 1955, he founded the Sisters of the Divine Spirit, an American religious congregation of home and foreign missionaries, whose services included teaching, visiting homes, and assisting in social work. He was devoted to the Holy Eucharist and Our Lady. He wrote more than 30 books and 75 pamphlets.

5 Lawrence G. Lovasik *The Basic Book of the Eucharist* (Manchester, N.H. Sophia Inst. Press, 1960), 206; Also by Fr. Lovasik, see *Mary My Hope, Blessed Sacrament Novenas, Our Lady in Catholic life.*

Prayer of Pope St. John Paul II

Come then, good Shepherd, bread divine,
Still show to us thy mercy sign;
Oh, feed us, still keep us thine;
So we may see thy glories shine
in fields of immortality.

O thou, the wisest, mightiest, best,
Our present food, our future rest,
Come, make us each thy chosen guest,
Co-heirs of thine, and comrades blest
With saints whose dwelling is with thee.

***Ecclesia de Eucharistia,* n. 62**

Chapter 5 Posture 101

Entering a Catholic Church

As one can observe today, coming to Mass and entering the church, as with other activities … our gestures often are meaningless or non-existent.

This is just an external manifestation of our internal loss in belief in the Real Presence.

Bodily posture is related to emotions and attitude, both of which connect with belief. Therefore, as we probe deeper into the need for greater reverence, let's begin with a basic practice. How do we enter a Catholic Church?

There have been many practices in the past that reinforced what we believe that have now disappeared. One of these is the way we conduct ourselves when we enter the church. We touched on the subject when we covered decorum, but it requires further discussion.

Is it not fitting or appropriate to make an act of reverence, to genuflect or to bow, along with the use of holy water when entering a Catholic church?

Remember, Moses and the burning bush? Exodus 3: 4-5:

Remove the sandals from your feet, for the place where you stand is holy ground. I am the God of your father, he continued, *the God of Abraham, the God of Isaac, the God of Jacob.*

This needs to be addressed in this ongoing revival. We need to revive and restore this practice.

Like Moses, are we not entering holy ground and holy space, when we enter a Catholic church?

Is not the whole Christ truly, really, and substantially present in the main church tabernacle?

But outward signs of reverence when entering the Church to acknowledge Christ's presence, such as sacred silence, and genuflecting, or making a bow have become increasingly absent these past 50 years.

If you attended Mass prior to 1970, everyone genuflected or at least bowed entering the church, while blessing themselves with holy water. These were ways Catholics "removed their sandals" and acknowledged we were on holy ground and before the presence of the Lord. Entering the church should still involve these two actions.

The removal of holy water during COVID has all but destroyed this practice, where fewer Catholics now avail themselves of this important sacramental. In some cases, the holy water fonts are still missing and just a baptismal font exists. Many will pass by due to its inconvenient location as they enter or depart and not avail themselves of holy water in this receptacle.

We need to be reminded.

We know the guidelines require us to genuflect when entering the pew, or at least a reverent bow when passing in front of the tabernacle. So the point here is, of course, to restore an act or gesture when we enter our churches. The Real Presence of Jesus Christ is there. Also upon leaving, to turn and face the tabernacle with a bow or sign of the Cross.

The opening of the book of Revelation comes to mind, where the Apostle John encounters Christ, the God Man, and falls flat on his face, the same Christ he ate and spoke with every day.

If we do recognize this as a major issue, then we must adjust our catechesis accordingly, but also our pedagogical methods.

It should certainly be in the forefront in what we teach and how we act.
We must not only believe, we must ACT like we believe. We don't act like we believe.

Acting out what we believe reinforces what we believe and influences others who don't believe.

The <u>OPTICS</u> like this are exactly what the bishops mention in their PILLAR FOUR. One need only sit in the back of a Catholic Church and watch people coming and going before and after Mass. Not knowing any better, you would think those attending Mass are merely attending a sporting event or some other secular gathering.

If a non-Catholic attended Mass and was watching, would he or she believe that Catholics entering truly believe that they're entering a space where the Son of the living God, the Creator of the universe is really and truly present? See Discussion.

Discussion

Msgr. Charles Pope

"Have We Lost Reverence in Church These Days?" [1]

The Monsignor appears in radio, newspapers, blogs, videos, lectures, and social media.
From the National Catholic Register. Accessed July 17, 2013.

"Almost no one dresses in any special way for Church these days. "Extreme casual" would seem to be the norm of the day, the look found in most parishes. Most people don't even think to change their clothes for church, there is a "go as you are" mentality.

Further, other signs of entering the Church such as sacred silence, and genuflecting are increasingly absent [as "before 1970"]. As a young boy and teenager, I had special Sunday shoes, hard black ones, and would not dream of going to church in jeans or a t-shirt. We were expected to wear pressed trousers, a button down shirt and tie, along with a jacket in the cooler months. The ladies all wore dresses and veils ... Church was a special place. Mass was a sacred occasion. On entering Church we were expected to maintain a sacred silence, and upon entering, to bless ourselves with Holy Water and genuflect on entering our pew. Silent prayer was expected of one prior to Mass.

These were the ways we "removed our sandals" and acknowledged we were on holy ground and before the Presence of the Lord ... I will not even argue that all the old traditions should return, even though I would like that. But at least we ought to recover some way of signifying that we are on holy ground and before the presence of the Holy One of Israel, the Lord of glory. [Some say] all this "stuffiness" will "turn people off." But of course Mass isn't just about pleasing people, it is about adoring the Lord who is worthy of our praise and our reverence **...** the bottom line seems to be that there ought to be some behavior that we fulfill the adoration of God to "*Remove your sandals for the ground on which you stand is holy, I am the God of your fathers.*"

Loss in the Sense of the Sacred

As Msgr. Pope suggested, the issue of how we enter the church is tied to one of the major issues facing the Church today that is substantiated statistically in many surveys: the loss of belief in the Real Presence of Jesus Christ in the Holy Eucharist. It is in turn closely tied to the *loss in the sense of the sacred.*
Msgr. Pope, quoting Cardinal Robert Sarah:

... it is no surprise that the disfiguration and profanation of the temples of our bodies has been extended to the temples of stone which are our church buildings. And to many places, the sanctuary is consecrated to God, an alternative [that has been turned into] soup kitchens, places for convivial meetings, or concert halls and cultural centers. Christians enter a church for the liturgical celebration, how many acknowledge the real presence of Christ in the tabernacle and honor him with a genuflection accompanied by a moment of prayer.

It bears repeating. If we do recognize that this as a major issue, then we must adjust our catechesis accordingly, but also our pedagogical methods. It should certainly be in the forefront in what we teach and how we act. We must not only believe, *we must act like we believe.* Too many don't act like they believe.

Acting like we believe reinforces what we do believe and that influences others that don't believe. There have been many practices in the past that reinforced what we believe that have now disappeared, and one of these is the way we conduct ourselves when we enter the church and our practices before, during, and after Mass as well (to be addressed later).

Entering the church should involve two actions, making an act of reverence as we enter sacred ground, and the use of the important sacramental: holy water which is closely connected and has also fallen from disuse prompted in part by the COVID restrictions, eroding its use by the faithful even further.

Are the above concerns real?

One need only sit in the back of a Catholic Church and watch people coming and going before and after Mass. Not knowing any better, one would think those attending Mass are merely attending a secular gathering. ***We must reestablish the sense of the sacred in our parishes, especially for what is about to take place at Mass.***

---

1 NCR July 17, 2013. "Have we Lost Reverence in Church These Days?" Condensed here: nhttps://blog.adw.org/2013/07/have-we-lost-reverence-in-church-these-days-how-can-we-recover-it/. Accessed July 5, 2025.

The "Optics" Matter

Recall from the introduction, Pillar Four, and the USCCB mention of the importance of the optics.

… using a specific example of genuflecting before the tabernacle as a way of outwardly starting conversations and a witness visually to others of what we believe.

The author did not say this. A priest did not say this. The USCCB said it!

In short ... the next time you arrive for Mass, presume that there is someone in there watching. Perhaps it's a non-Catholic or maybe an unbelieving fallen away Catholic. He or she knows that we believe in the Real Presence.

How do you convince that person? You don't know who he or she is.
You cannot go over to him and start quoting biblical verses.

The only thing you have is yourself.

What postures and gestures can you take to show them that you truly believe?
… the way you enter the church, blessing yourself, and especially the way you receive Holy Communion. He is watching.

As someone remarked:

"I spoke with a Muslim friend who said that if he believed the Eucharist was the Body of Christ, he would crawl on his belly to receive it."

At Communion, as we receive our Lord, our response is "Amen," that is, "so be it." By saying the word Amen, we are affirming that we truly believe it is Jesus Christ. We say it. But ...

It's not enough to believe, we must act like we believe!
Actions speak, louder than words!

ACTION POINTS

As noted … sit in the back of one of our Catholic churches and observe how people enter and exit.

What are some ideas to keep the noise down?
It might be a suggestion by the pastor, it might be praying the Rosary or other prayers before and after the Mass, or it may be by playing Gregorian Chants while the congregation is entering. You create the *sounds* of a sacred space we are entering.

Discuss, as a priest noted:

In our society today, belief in the "equality of all" is spilling over to belief also that one should not bow to anyone, God not excepted. However, this in practice does not hold when certain people "do not want to share, and do not want others to have." If we cannot prove that the there is absolute equality of all people, how can anyone refuse to honor God without thinking that in doing so is taking away one's sense of equality?

Notes

Chapter 6 Change of Posture for Communion

Brief Historical Review

FACT:

Communion on the tongue is still normative …

Communion in the hand was granted by concession or permission only.

The full history is complicated. We must go back 60 years to understand the origin and circumstances surrounding the concession for Holy Communion in the hand vs. the tongue, to the period just following the Second Vatican Council. Fact: this was not part of the post conciliar liturgical reform. We often hear the claim that these changes were the result of Vatican II … in the "spirit of Vatican II." There is no spirit of Vatican II except what the Vatican II documents actually say. [1]

Vatican II had nothing to do with this issue. When the Council closed, Communion kneeling and receiving on the tongue were still normative. Keep in mind, until then, Communion was received kneeling and on the tongue for roughly 1500 years. We will address reception of Communion in the early Church later.

Communion in the hand, contrary to the norms, was not even talked about either at the Vatican Council or in the liturgical reform movement. It is rooted in the post-conciliar period in the rebellious dioceses of northern Europe, especially by the mid 1960's. Some countries began receiving in the hand without permission by Rome. And although Pope Paul VI immediately communicated (beginning in 1965) to those bishops that they needed to return immediately to the only legal manner of receiving, that is, on the tongue, he was ignored.[2]

The Pontiff sought to address this with his 1969 Instruction *Memoriale Domini* (MD) which was intended to reaffirm the benefits of communion on the tongue and restrict this practice through an indult only to the rebellious dioceses in which there had not been success in curbing the abuse. In a related memorandum by the MD editor Archbishop Bugnini…

It was considered a liturgical abuse. **The practice was considered "very questionable and dangerous" and there was "the danger of weakening the faith of the people in the Eucharistic presence."** [3]

Weakening the faith? Weakening the faith in what?
Weakening the faith and belief in the Real Presence, which was what the three year USCCB Eucharistic Revival was all about!!!

Pope Paul VI (in MD):

> ***A change in a matter of such moment, based on a most ancient and venerable tradition, does not merely affect discipline. It carries certain dangers with it, which may arise from the new manner of administering Holy Communion: the danger of a loss of reverence for the august sacrament of the altar; profanation, adulterating the true doctrine.***

The change in the practice of receiving Communion not only was not willed by the Holy See, but it was never part of the post conciliatory liturgical reform that was then in progress. It was only tolerated by the Holy Father by an indult granted as a consequence of the insistent, tenacious pressure of some episcopal conferences particularly in countries with large Protestant populations. Furthermore, the indult was granted only after the practice had been extended in a completely abusive way, and which did not take into account the denunciations and prohibitions of Rome until the point when Paul VI finally concluded that it was impossible to resist anymore.[3]

What is an Indult?

> ***Indults are general faculties, granted by the Holy See to bishops and others, of doing something not permitted by the common law. General needs, peculiar local conditions, the impossibility of applying to Rome in individual cases, etc., are sufficient reasons for making these concessions.*** (Ref. Canon Law, New Advent)

It spread to the U.S. eventually in the 1970s.[4] The abuse was already occurring (with no choice but to tolerate it, with fear of a violent reaction) but would be able to request an indult *"ad normam"* (according to the law) for Communion in the hand. The U.S. bishops were able to achieve a 2/3 majority vote in favor of requesting it despite many of the U.S. bishops were kept out of the discussions, some were also not present to vote.

Importantly, the 1969 Instruction *Memoriale Domini* **(Appendix Chapter 6)** which governs the indult permitting communion in the hand does not equate the two forms receiving Communion. **Communion in the hand should not be imposed in a way that would exclude the traditional manner**. In fact, Communion on the tongue is still considered the most consonant way to receive the Eucharist, while **Communion in the hand is permitted, provided that certain precautions are observed, such as checking to see if any fragments of the Host remain *<u>on the palm of the hand</u>*…**

> ***… diligent carefulness about the fragments of consecrated bread which the Church has always recommended: What you have allowed to drop, think of it as though you had lost one of your own members … No matter which method is adopted, one will be careful not to allow any fragment of the host to fall....***

Does anyone do that today?

Fragments wiped from floor by author with a black towel after three Masses, typically vacuumed up.

The *theology of the fragments*[5] is a corollary of the Church's teaching on transubstantiation. Every fragment is still the Body, Blood, Soul and Divinity of Jesus Christ. Consequently, the governing document for the indult that was granted to the United States requires care of the fragments which end up in the communicant's hands. If not, where will they end up? Most of the fragments will end up on the floor to be vacuumed up. These are the same fragments that the priest cleans from the sacred vessels post-communion on the altar. So it cannot be considered scrupulosity.

Initially, in the 1970's, the paten was still used but over these past 50 years, this practice has fallen in disuse in most parishes.

Communion on the tongue vs. the hand, as well as the problem of the fragments and how to take care of them will be covered in subsequent chapters.

Ecclesial documents (e.g. *Redemptionis Sacramentum* n. 91) requires that communicants have the ability to receive Communion in the traditional manner, kneeling, and on the tongue. *The disappearance of communion rails was never mandated, and the current practice of communicants coming forward standing in a line becomes an obstacle making it difficult for those who want to kneel.*

Kneeling vs standing will be covered also in subsequent chapters.

Resources, Notes

1 Most Rev. Juan Rodolfo Laise, *Holy Communion,* (Boonville, N.Y., Preserving Christian Publications, 2018) 1-5. Also notes here from Preface and Introduction, thru page 21.

2 Ibid., ii, 2.

3 Ibid., 2-3, 38-39, 58-59, 99. Extensively covered here by Laise. Besides quotes here from Archbishop Bugnini, also the quote from Cardinal Gut, Prefect of the Congregation of Divine Worship.

4 Not all countries have an indult. Consequently, still receive Communion kneeling and on the tongue.

5 Rev Richard W. Gilsdorf , "The Doctrine of the Fragments", *Homiletic and Pastoral Review*, Feb. 1980.

See Appendix, Chapter 6. *The Theology of the Fragments.*

Fishing
Allowed
NO BOATING
ALLOWED

Kneeling
Allowed
No Kneelers
Allowed

DISCUSSION

It would be useful to review Juan Rodolfo's Book *Holy Communion* through page 21. See bibliography.

To establish the fact that there are fragments on the floor, one need only wipe the floor where communion is distributed.

This practice probably not recommended in general, but people have responded by caring for the fragments that fall.

Use a small black folded towel. Dampen it. And at the proper time during the course of the week, before the floors of your parish have been vacuumed, wipe the floor up front where Communion is distributed.

The number and size may vary. It may be three or four, or it may be 10, sometimes larger pieces, sometimes just small fragments, but all of which are the Body, Soul, Blood and Divinity of Jesus Christ.

After wiping them up, consume them with the tip of your tongue. Preserve the small towel in a Ziploc bag.

You can also photograph them and show them to your pastor.

There is often an outward denial that this problem exists. It establishes the fact that Pope Paul VI was correct related to Communion in the hand.

ACTION POINTS

At your parish, if communion in the hand is widely distributed with no patens, be assured there will be fragments on the floor.
So what is the solution?

- **Obviously, reestablish the use of the paten**
- **Remind people to check their hands for fragments and to consume**
- **Encourage communion on the tongue**
- **Remind people not to consume the Host off to the side**
- **Volunteer to wipe the floor area after Mass**

Notes

Prayer of St. John Chrysostom

Grant, O Lord, that we may partake
of the precious Body and Blood
to the sanctification, enlightening
and strengthening of our soul and body,
to the ease of the burden of our many sins,
to our safeguarding
from all the snares of the evil one,
to the victory over our sinful and evil habits,
to the modification of our passions,
to the fulfillment of your commandments,
to the increase in me of your divine grace,
and to the inheritance of your kingdom.
Amen

My friend, if Jesus stood in front of you now, you would kneel, believe me, you'd put your face right on the ground, because suddenly you would know the awesome presence of God. It's not a matter of kneeling or standing. I think this whole big deal about standing instead of kneeling it's not a matter of a rubric …

It's a matter of faith.

If you believe this is a cookie like I've been told, then you might as well stand. In fact, you can stand on your head for a cookie. But it's not what it is. It's the Body, Blood, Soul and Divinity of the Lord God, who humbled himself to become a piece of bread.

Are you telling me that you are so proud that you are not going to kneel for that occasion? Are we so proud in our hearts? Are we so full of sin, we're like a stone that we refuse to bend the knee?

You know what scripture says? Huh? Let me tell you. It says, "every knee shall bend on the earth, and under the earth, at the very name of Jesus, let alone his presence.

That my dear friend is my humble opinion.

Mother Angelica

Chapter 7 Communion Standing vs. Kneeling

Responding to the arguments for standing ...

<u>**USCCB**</u> **PILLAR 5**: While standing in the U.S. is considered the norm (GIRM 160) ... *appropriate reverence during the act of receiving Holy Communion ... standing, kneeling, in the hand, or the tongue are all acceptable* (also see Canon 843.1).

While standing, kneeling, in the hand, or the tongue are now all ***acceptable*** are any of these more ***appropriate?*** Which do we choose? This is what we will now examine.

First up ... the practice of standing. When introduced the altar rails began to disappear. Removing the altar rails did much to discourage kneeling ... perhaps to legitimize standing. We hear the following arguments ...

ARGUMENT ONE: [1]

Kneeling was medieval ... The early Christians prayed standing. Standing signifies the resurrected Christ ... it is the most appropriate attitude and posture for a Christian in line with Vatican II. Standing is also safer.

RESPONSE ONE: [2]

Is all that right? Well .... not really. *Praying* when standing is one thing, a classic posture for prayer in the Old Testament or at Easter (12th century), the posture for Communion for hundreds of years including much of the early Church is another. We should also realize that what is an expression of veneration in one period can be an expression of blasphemy in another. Standing was not imposed by Vatican II but emerged in the liturgical reform period afterwards. Kneeling still prevailed.

Kwasniewski: You think people who have been kneeling for 1000 years suddenly, came to their senses, got on their feet, and thought: "We're now doing it like the early Christians did?" Most parishioners are not aware that they are returning to some original early form of worship. They simply get up, and may say to themselves: "kneeling wasn't such a serious business after all." And in doing so, the deeper spiritual significance of the Presence of Christ is often lost. Even if we all affirm it explicitly.

YES .. Most Catholics receive the Eucharist reverently, standing or kneeling.

But remember the optics. *Remember again the objectives,*

Do we <u>ACT</u> like we believe?

Are our acts of reverence telling others we truly believe?

While one kneels with the primary desire to be more reverent and not to draw attention to oneself, it certainly can become an outward sign which may inspire others with the same desire to kneel as well.

RESPONSE TWO:

Yes. We do already observe the practice of kneeling. This includes entering the pew, and two times set aside for Eucharistic Adoration or solemn exposition, and when the Host is placed in a monstrance. Because in the western tradition, *kneeling is the most appropriate response to the Real Presence of the Lord.*

300s.

1400s,

1600s,

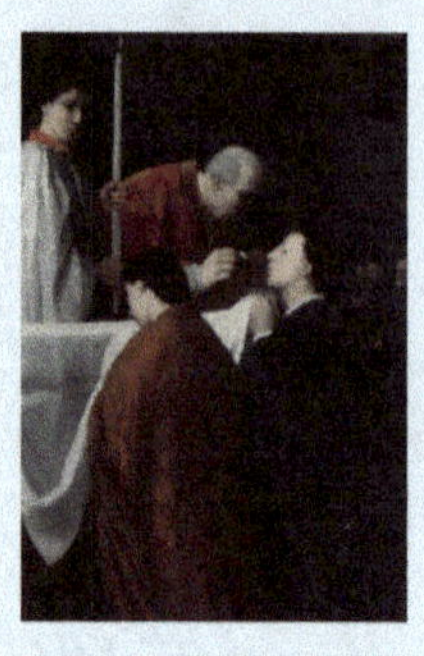

1800s,

1900s

The posture for Communion in the early Church and for hundreds of years ... was kneeling!

This is why we kneel for the Eucharistic prayer and when the miracle of transubstantiation takes place. Well, if kneeling for these times is appropriate, why are we not kneeling for the most intimate moment of Communion? Biblically– like the magi, like Jarius (Lk 8:41), like Mary of Bethany, and John (Rev 1:17), we *know* whose presence we are in. We've come to adore, to receive, to abide, and to love. [3]

Biblical Support

Mk 2:11

Lk 8:41

Rev. 1:17

As Popular Author Fr. Dwight Longenecker notes: [4]

"One of the most instrumental factors in developing reverence in Mass is how we receive Communion. While the faithful can certainly be reverent standing and receiving Communion in the hand, while standing, no one can disagree that receiving Communion on the tongue while kneeling is more reverent."

Why is this? First, because kneeling in our western culture is an intrinsic act of devotion, homage, and worship. This is true no matter what the context.

- Knights kneel to receive knighthood from the queen
- Bride and groom kneel to receive a nuptial blessing
- Everyone kneels in the presence of royalty or even some dignitaries

To receive Communion kneeling is a sign of belief that the eucharistic Host is the Real Presence of Christ's Body and Blood, and a sign that you are intent not to profane in any way, the Body of Christ.

The visual impact, that is the optics, are massive to unbelievers, and also to the youth *and young adults* where we find statistically the greatest number of non-believers (80%).

"Well …. we have good catechesis"…
"We're teaching them it's the Body and Blood of Jesus"
That's not enough!!! Actions speak louder than words!

Many know what the Church teaches but there is still doubt, especially when the Eucharist is handled as if it is regular common food.

If we treat it as mere common food,
then it will be seen as merely everyday food …
That couldn't possibly be Jesus! Just a symbol!

Pope Benedict 16th, Homily, May 22, 2008:

> *"Kneeling and adoration before the Eucharist is the most valid and radical remedy against the idolatries of yesterday and today."*

Why not honor our Lord and God with our heart, soul, mind, AND … BODY in the midst of a Church and culture that reject the supernatural? This is the great mystery of our faith!

We are body-soul creatures! Body posture matters!!

With the stated goal of restoring reverence and belief in the Real Presence, should we not revert to the long-standing practice of ***kneeling***?

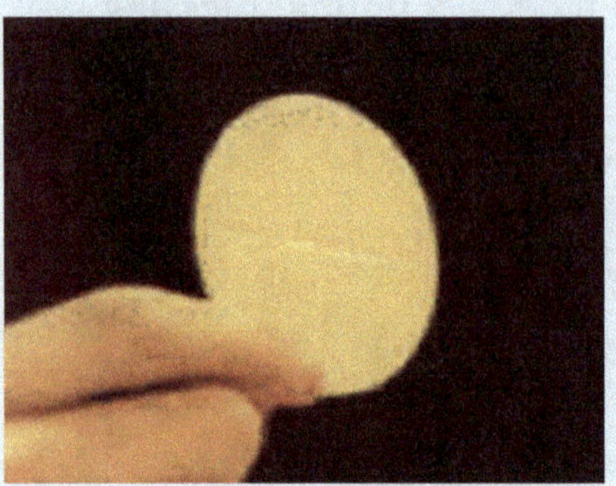

We kneel before dignitaries, kings and queens … why not *kneel* before God, Christ the King?

Kneeling to Receive Communion

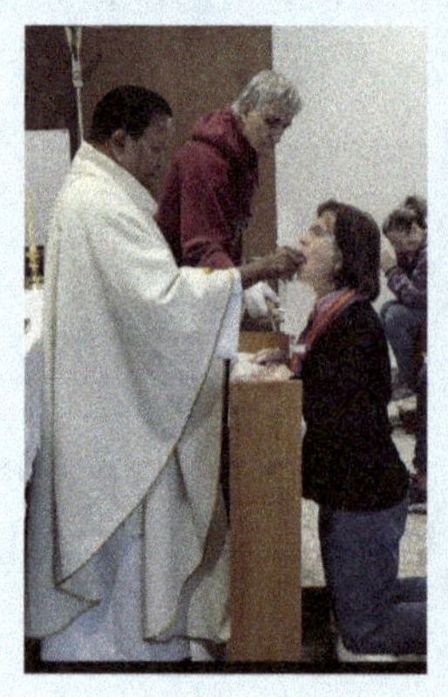

Why do we kneel? Why is kneeling more ***appropriate***?

The kneeling posture is still allowed in *Novus Ordo* rite. While the guidelines do not prohibit one from kneeling, for most parishes, provisions *enabling* people to conveniently kneel are absent, making it difficult for some to support themselves to kneel on the floor. There is also the pressure of a moving communion line, which makes the communicant feel self-conscience, and *uneasy*. Most "follow the crowd" even with other gestures and postures during Mass.

Absence/removal of communion rails has had an impact. But even parishes in older churches that still have communion rails, they are often not used. Nor are portable kneelers made available, making it almost impossible to kneel. And despite the ecclesiastical guidelines, sadly there are some parishes that even prohibit kneeling.

Kneeling as an Expression of Humility[5]

Kneeling (Greek: proskyneō) does not come from any culture – it comes from the Bible and its knowledge of God. If we are to worship God, not merely out of routine or habit, but a loving intelligence, we need to understand *why we are doing what we do.* And so, *why do we kneel* or also genuflect as the USCCB expressed in Pillar Four? Why is this posture so important, so meaningful, that we use it at Mass as during the eucharistic prayer and was once the *universal* custom when we receive Holy Communion?

The posture for Communion for 1300 years and in the early Church was kneeling:

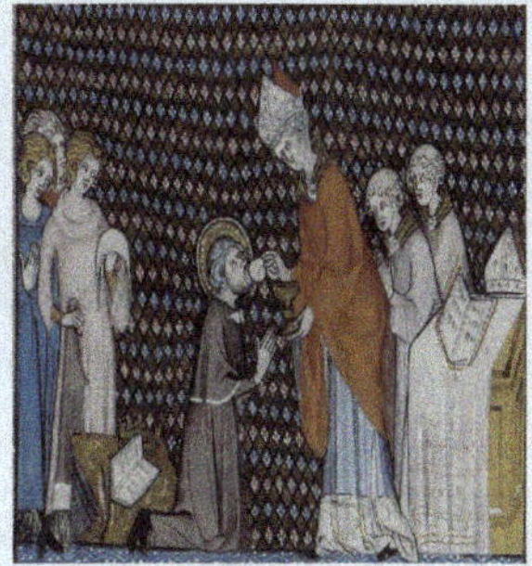

Kwasniewski:[6] Thomas Aquinas' commentary on the epistle to the Ephesians teaches kneeling is a symbol of humility, and for two reasons.

First a person "belittles himself in a certain way when he genuflects and subjects himself to the one he genuflects before. In such a way, he recognizes his own weakness and insignificance."

Second, "physical strength is present in the knees, and so bending them we confess openly to our lack of strength."

Thus, external, physical symbols are shown to God for the purpose of renewing and spiritually training the inner soul, as in …

I bend the knee of my heart, and for every knee shall bow to me: and every tongue shall swear (Is 45:24).

We must retrain the inner self with humility before the infinite holiness of God.

"In spite of the illusions fostered by a modern democracy, we are *not* equals before Jesus Christ, our Lord; He is our Lord and Master, and we are His disciples, servants, and adorers." [7]

"Yes, He lovingly calls us his friends; but He's not just any friend, He is the Lord of heaven and earth who has called us out of darkness into His marvelous light (1 Pt 2:9)."

God … "deserves (and rewards) our absolute, self surrender, which no creature can demand or receive. This is why kneeling, within a tradition that has long expressed and cultivated the attitude of humility, is no more an incidental or external feature that we can take or leave." **We are not doing it to call attention to ourselves.** "It is part of our fundamental spiritual discipline. Kneeling is a vivid and heartfelt expression of worship, of the adoration that is due to our Lord and God."

It may take some courage to kneel. See Appendix, page 117.

There is plenty of scriptural support that to prostrate oneself, or to kneel down before the majesty of the divine presence, in humble adoration, was a habit of reverence that Israel always practiced in the presence of the Lord. [8]

Also in the New Testament. St. Peter kneeling before Jesus (Lk 5:8) and John kneeling in the book of Revelation before the divine presence of our Lord.

Phil 2:10. *At the name of Jesus, every knee shall bend ...* Of course here we have at Holy Communion more than just the name of Jesus ... we have Jesus himself!

Cardinal Robert Sarah encourages kneeling:[9] *"The greatness and nobility of man, as well as the highest expression of his love for his Creator, consists in kneeling before God. Jesus himself prayed on his knees in the presence of the Father ..."*

Then, it follows, with kneeling still allowed, the Church has taught that the Eucharist, the bread and wine substantiated into the Body and Blood of Christ, God in our midst has to be received with awe, with the greatest reverence, and with an attitude of humble adoration ... *ON OUR KNEES!*

And it is safe. Claims that it is safer to stand have no basis and have no statistics to support this. And with kneelers you anticipate the person in front will kneel.

And so, if you are able, we should not hesitate to kneel! Don't worry about holding up the communion line! It takes some courage! You may encourage others.

You of course can kneel with no kneeler, kneel on one knee if you have to so you to support yourself perhaps inspiring others to kneel and the parish to use kneelers. But Kneel!

God gave us souls and bodies, and He wants us to worship him in our souls interiorly and in our bodies exteriorly. ***"Worship is one of those fundamental acts that affects the whole of man, that is why bending the knee before the presence of the living God is something we cannot abandon."*** Cardinal Ratzinger (Quote ln Discussion, p 70).

Resources, Notes

1 Peter Kwasniewski, *The Holy Bread of Eternal Life, Restoring Eucharistic Reverence in an age of Impiety* (Manchester, N.H: Sophia Institute Press, 2020), 113. Much of this is from Dr. Kwasniewski.
2 Ibid., pp 112-113 (from Martin Mosebach).
3 Ibid., 91.
4 Ibid., 114, from his *Letters on the liturgy* (Brooklyn, N.Y.: Angelico Press, 2020), 51; cf.118,
5 Ibid., 89-91.
6 Ibid., 89-90.
7 Ibid., 90.
8 Ibid., 91. Referencing Cardinal Malcolm Ranjith.
9 Robert Cardinal Sarah,; *National Catholic Register*: https://www.ncregister.com/features/the-return-of-altar-rails Accessed July 6, 2025.

DISCUSSION

Acquiring the *Courage* to Kneel

In the Catholic tradition, kneeling when able during Mass is a profound act of belief and reverence. It is not merely a custom or ritual, but a living act of love that expresses our faith in the Real Presence of Jesus Christ in the Eucharist. Here is why kneeling requires courage:

- Showing reverence in a secular world: A society may have lost reverence for what is sacred. Kneeling during Mass is a visible sign of submission to God and an acknowledgment of the presence of the King of Kings, which can be countercultural.
- Overcoming perceived awkwardness: People may feel self-conscious or conspicuous when kneeling, especially if they are not used to it or if their parish has different liturgical practices. Remembering the profound meaning behind the action can give other people the courage to kneel. Installing kneelers also is a signal that if you wish to kneel, there is no problem. It is an *invitation* to kneel.

  Many do desire to kneel and often results acts of courage. Three actual examples are provided in Appendix, page 117.

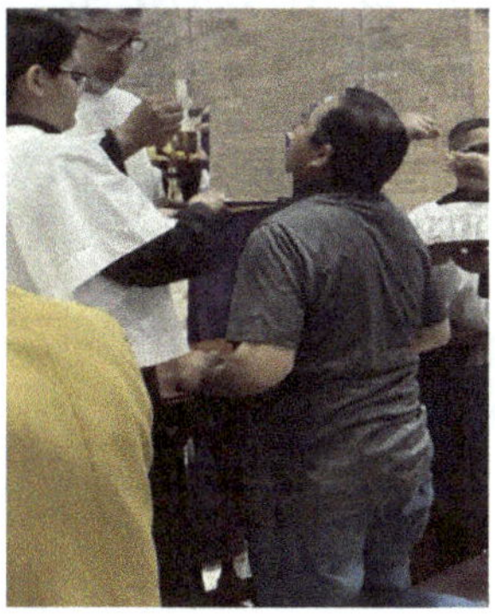

- Embracing humility and submission: Kneeling is a gesture of humility, recognizing that we are creatures before the Lord. It's a physical reminder that people depend on God. Our body, our posture, informs the mind, it informs the soul.

Kneeling is a sign of:

- Belief in the Eucharist: Kneeling expresses faith that the bread and wine are transformed into the Body, Blood, Soul, and Divinity of Jesus Christ during the Consecration.
- Adoration and worship: Our posture informs the mind. Kneeling is a posture of adoration and deep reverence for God, recognizing His supreme authority and holiness.
- Humility and penitence: Kneeling signifies humility before God and willingness to submit to Him.

Answering an objection:

Both kneeling and standing are equally reverent. What only matters is what's in the heart.

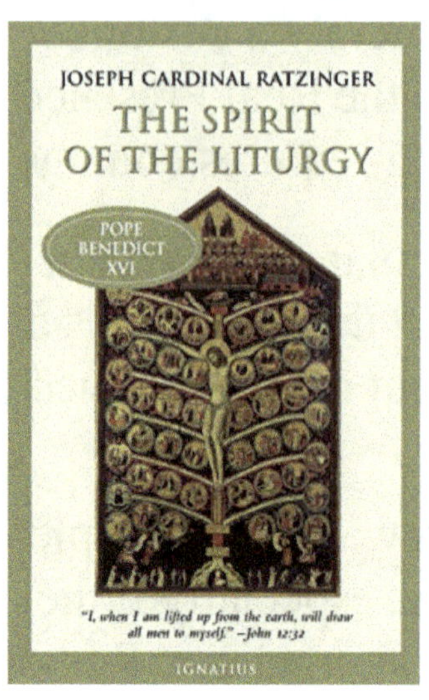

The bodily gesture itself is the bearer of the spiritual meaning, which is precisely that of worship. Without the worship, the bodily gesture would be meaningless, while the spiritual act must of its very nature, because of the psychosomatic unity of man, express itself in the bodily gesture. The two aspects are united in this one word [kneeling], because in a very profound way, they belong together. When kneeling becomes merely external, merely physical act, it becomes meaningless. On the other hand, when someone tries to take worship back into the purely spiritual realm and refuses to give it embodied form, the act of worship, evaporates, for what is purely spiritual, is inappropriate to the nature of man. Worship is one of those fundamental acts that affect the whole man. That is why bending the knee before the presence of the living God is something we cannot abandon.

Joseph Cardinal Ratzinger. "The Spirit of the Liturgy" p.190-191 (Commemorative Edition: pp. 204-205)

Comment:

Angels are entirely spiritual. They have no bodies and so it's entirely appropriate to them to worship God just spiritually. They have no other way to worship God. But God gave us souls and bodies, and He wants us to worship him in our souls interiorly and in our bodies exteriorly.

ACTION POINTS

We are permitted to receive Communion in the traditional manner … kneeling and on the tongue.

If we do not give our people the ability to kneel then we are not meeting the intent of the ecclesial documents that allows kneeling?

Do our parishes have provisions to enable people to kneel?

Discuss with other parishioners their desire to receive Communion kneeling.

While installing altar rails is on the rise, there is an alternate solution. Most parishes have portable kneelers and have now been installing them for Mass. **See Chapter 10.**

Notes

Come, then, good Shepherd, bread divine,
Still show to us thy mercy sign;
Oh, feed us, still keep us thine;
So we may see thy glories shine
in fields of immortality.

O thou, the wisest, mightiest, blest,
Our present food, our future rest,
Come, make us each thy chosen guest,
Co-heirs of thine, and comrades blest
With Saints who's dwelling is with thee.

Thomas Aquinas

Chapter 8 Communion in the Hand vs. the Tongue

Arguments for in the Hand

Where did Communion in the hand come from? What are the concerns?

We already explored in Chapter 6, the liturgical reform movement and this practice erupting in northern Europe which eventually spread to the U.S.... and Pope Paul VI's efforts to restrict this practice (see Chapter 6).

As will now be discussed, not only has this contributed to the loss in belief in the Real Presence, but also in the careless handling of the Eucharist and the fragments, a concern expressly stated in the document *Memoriale Domini* which required **... *the diligent care which the Church has always commended for the very fragments of the consecrated bread will be maintained.***

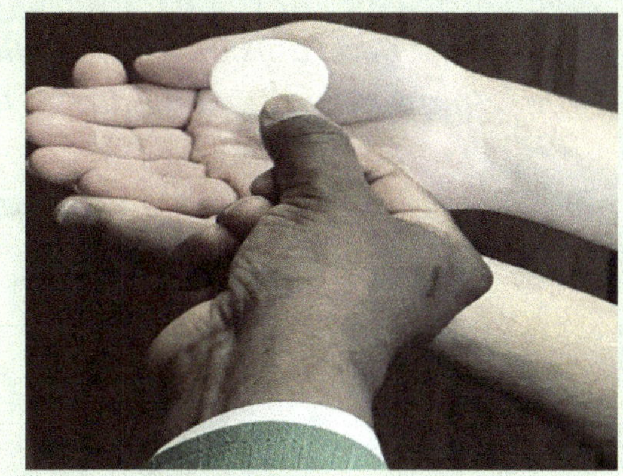

How has this practice been justified?

<u>ARGUMENT ONE</u>

Proponents of Communion in the hand have justified their position by finding evidence in the early Church of a similar practice ...

The early Christians are supposed to have received Communion in their hands. What is irreverent about the faithful making their hands into a throne for the host? [1]

Is this right? Where does this come from?

The claim is that Communion in the hand is taken from St Cyril of Jerusalem and so the return to Communion in the hand is therefore nothing more that an ancient practice that was restored with Vatican II.

We often hear now too: "hold your hands out like it is an altar [or throne]" the Host to be placed on your hands as such.

Response:

In reference to Saint Cyril, this claim is taken from his Catechetical Lecture 23, 348 AD par. N. 21; Full text: [2]

21. In approaching therefore, come NOT with your wrists extended, or your fingers spread; but make your left hand a throne for the right, as for that which is to receive a King. And having hollowed your palm, receive the Body of Christ, saying over it, Amen.
So then after having carefully hallowed your eyes by the touch of the Holy Body, partake of it; giving heed lest you lose any portion thereof; for whatever you lose, is evidently a loss to you as it were from one of your own members. For tell me, if any one gave you grains of gold, would you not hold them with all carefulness, being on your guard against losing any of them, and suffering loss?
Will you not then much more carefully keep watch, that not a crumb fall from you of what is more precious than gold and precious stones?

Sketch from patrology specialists, possible more extreme "bow" body posture …[3]

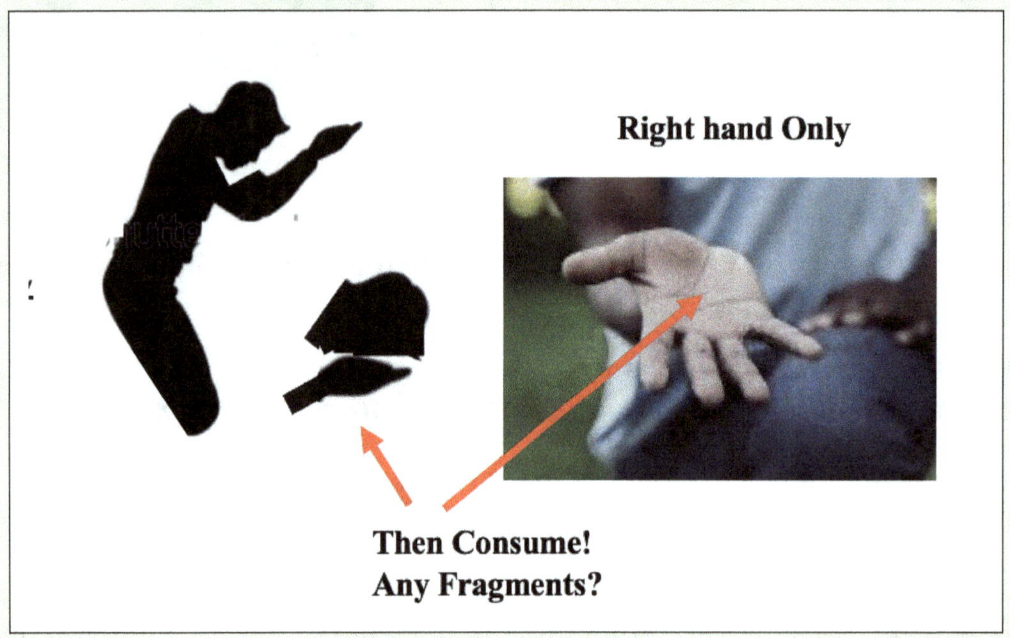

Several things to observe as taught by St Cyril:

1. Care for the Fragments: The extreme care that *not a speck of the consecrated bread should be lost – that would be like a mutilation of one's body, a loss of something more precious than any created thing as in handling gold dust.* It was, in fact, this very emphasis on the immense care to be taken toward the Eucharist [the fragments], together with an ever deepening appreciation of the sheer magnitude of so a divine gift, that led the Church over time to abandon in the hand and prefer convenient directly in the mouth on the tongue.

2. It is significant too that the Eucharist be laid on the **right hand,** not the less valued left-hand, and then the communicant consumes the host directly by the mouth off the palm of the hand, ***prohibited to touch with the fingers.***

Do we observe this today when receiving in our hands?

3. Notice: The communicant likely was not fully upright … an accentuated bow.

Do we bow profoundly today when standing and receiving in our the hands?

Much of this is backed up by religious artwork of the early Church which also depicted a communion cloth draped over or under the hands. The purpose was so that they would not directly touch the Holy Sacrament, and any fragments could easily be gathered. [4]

So –

While proponents of Communion in the hand have justified their position by finding evidence in the early Church of a similar practice, in this case with St. Cyril, we find they not only misrepresent the actual early practice by ignoring other important parts that conflict with current practices (as in touching with the fingers), only selecting the parts that support their position. [5]

If we're going to revert to a particular liturgical practice of the primitive Church, then why not all of it? How about paragraph 22 by Cyril concerning the consumption of the wine …[6]

22. *Then after you have partaken of the Body of Christ draw near also to the Cup of His Blood; not stretching forth your hands, but bending, and saying with an air of worship and reverence, "Amen," hallow yourself by partaking also of the Blood of Christ. And while the moisture is still upon your lips, touch it with your hands, and hallow your eyes and brow and the other organs* …

If we are going to follow the practice of Saint Cyril, then why are we ignoring the rest? Are we dampening our fingers with the wine on our lips, now with Blood of Christ, and touch the "eyes and brow, and other organs?"

And what of the fragments?
Who today is checking their hands?

For Cyril the left hand only acted as a paten, never to touch the Host.
Which hand do we use? Where are the patens today to collect the fragments?

Left or Right?

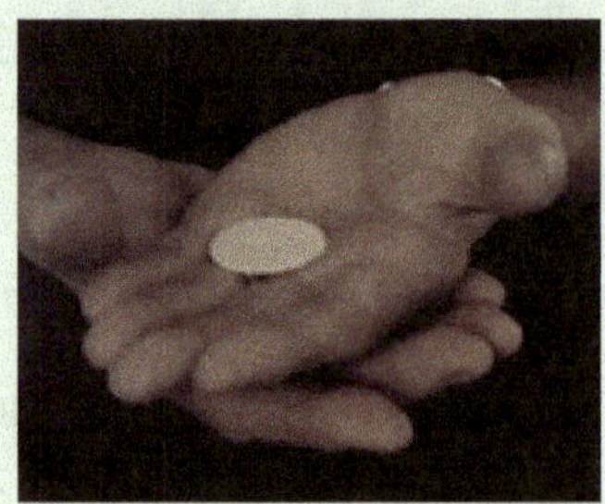

In Summary:

The practice had a different form in ancient times than it does today. There is no distinction as to which hand we receive the Host nor in touching it with our fingers:

The common practice today is to receive the Eucharist standing upright, taking it with either hand. If by the left, this is something which, symbolically, the Church Fathers would have found horrific – how can the Holy of Holies be taken with the left? [7]

Then, today, the faithful take and touch the host directly with their fingers and then put the Host in the mouth: this gesture has never been known in the entire history of the Catholic Church.

The practice in the hand was promoted by John Calvin who did not believe in the Real Presence and treated it as ordinary bread.

Author Klaus Gamber: *Catholics are now breathing the thin air of Calvinistic sterility.*

Consequently, **the liturgical practice expressed by St. Cyril was abandoned by the Church and a primary example of *organic development in the liturgy,*** which pursues the implications of an original belief or attitude until the external expression, most perfectly reflects, and inculcates that belief or attitude. [8]

Reinstating Communion in the hands ignores the legitimate and profound liturgical development under the guidance of the Holy Spirit. The artificial return to a much earlier, but long since discontinued practice – and one that now, reappearing in a very different context carries with it overtones of casualness and lack of faith in the Real Presence – it is an example of the **error of *antiquarianism* condemned in 1947 by Pius 12th in *Mediator Dei.*** [9]

In short: the ancient record bears witness to belief in attitudes that would, over time, develop into the long-standing Communion praxis of both in the Latin West and Byzantine East. In the West, Communion on the tongue while kneeling, is the natural and suitable result of St. Cyril's Eucharistic piety!!!

The attempt to turn back the clock to antiquity can be deceptive and unknowingly misrepresented. Most Catholics are unfamiliar with eucharistic practices in the early Church. The early Christians did not practice Communion on the hand the way we do today. More related arguments follow.

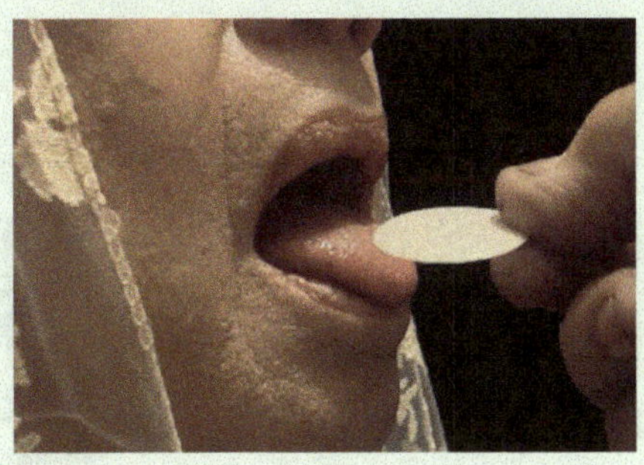

ARGUMENT TWO [10]

For the first thousand years of the Church Communion was given in the hand only. John Calvin and the heresy of Gnosticism that the human body was evil, argued: 'You aren't good enough to touch the Body of Christ with your hand, only with your tongue?' as if ***the tongue is holier than the hand****. When someone is Baptized or Confirmed their entire being baptized or confirmed not just their tongue. They are anointed and consecrated to Christ, their entire body mind and spirit.*

What do we say to this?

Response (Kwasnieski):

1. We already have evidence from the first millennium, of placing the host directly into the mouth. There is even indications of it at the Last Supper (see below).
2. Early Christians did not practice Communion in the hand in the way as we do (e.g. Cyril)… our way today is novel and removes the aura of sacredness.
3. The custom of receiving directly into the mouth, observed for well over 1000 years by all eastern western Christians, *has nothing to do with Calvin or Gnosticism or Jansenism*, but with humble and adoring reverence toward the body of Christ, and respect for the anointed hands of the priest. The custom also predominated for practical reasons: it is safer and more efficient.
4. The tongue, as a matter-of-fact, was especially blessed in the traditional rite of baptism, where a pinch of salt was placed on the tongue, with a prayer that looks ahead to the reception of Communion:

   Look graciously down on this Thy servant _N_ and as he tastes this first nutrient of salt, suffer him no longer to hunger for want of heavenly food, to the end that he may be always fervent in spirit, rejoicing in hope, always serving thy name.

"Lex orandi, lex credendi" … As we pray so too we believe.

"lex agendi, lex credendi," … as we put into practice, so too we believe!

There is an interdependent inseparability between belief and practice.

Eliminate the practice, you erode the belief.

ARGUMENT THREE [11]

Communion on the tongue indicates a lack of proper Eucharistic theology and is out of line and also ambiguous. Some through the years have made this claim in other ways, such as to say that Communion in the hand is a sign of spiritual maturity, or that Communion on the tongue reduces the lay faithful to infancy.

Such views (and others) significantly misrepresent the Church's disciplinary practice as to the reception of Holy Communion. Further, these views seem based on a sort of self-referential appeal to a notion that any views contrary are "flawed" in some vague sense.

Most of the Church's greatest saints never realized that they were infantile by receiving on the tongue. Furthermore, the Eastern Churches who administer the Eucharist under both species and only on the tongue are seemingly unaware that they have a lack of proper Eucharistic theology.

ARGUMENT FOUR

At the Last Supper: … the invitation of Jesus: "take and eat … take and drink" So "take" implies the hand. Is that right?

Response: [12]

In the Greek: it is *labete,* and Latin *accipiter* also means *receive.* And as some scholars point out, as reflected at the Last Supper, Jesus responding to Peter's request as to who would betray him, replied:

> *"it is he, for whom I shall dip the bread, and give it to him, and when he had dipped the bread he gave it to Judas…"*

Well, already dipped it cannot be taken with the hands, but rather it is received directly into the mouth. Like our customs of the day, such as the bride and the bride groom at a wedding when they feed cake to one another; and the Jews and the peoples of the east in general with a custom of taking food with one's hands and placing it directly in the mouth of the lover or the friend. So too, likely, Jesus at the last Supper, also represented in early biblical art.[13]

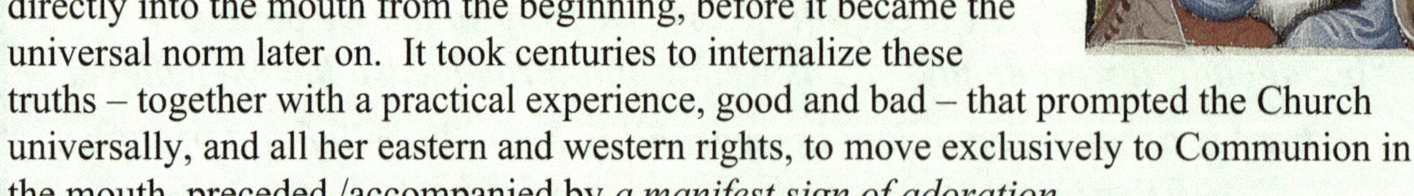

The conclusion to be drawn is, considering Jewish customs, not all Communion was given this way in ancient times, but rather we *cannot exclude* that Communion was at least sometimes given directly into the mouth from the beginning, before it became the universal norm later on. It took centuries to internalize these truths – together with a practical experience, good and bad – that prompted the Church universally, and all her eastern and western rights, to move exclusively to Communion in the mouth, preceded /accompanied by *a manifest sign of adoration.*

Arguments for Communion on the Tongue

Remembering again to keep our primary goal in focus, that is, *the Optics* …
To restore reverence and belief in the Real Presence …

Is receiving on the tongue the appropriate way to receive the Lord?

Rationale, as Kwasniewski notes: "It has centuries of unanimous practice in the east and the west behind it. Accordingly, then it must be considered a development guided by the Holy Spirit or else we have to conclude that the one true Church of Christ has gone off the rails in its second millennium." [14]

And if we believe that every part of that sacred Host is in fact, the Body, Blood, Soul and Divinity of Jesus Christ, then the distribution of the Holy Eucharist must be done as to prevent any dispersion or loss of fragments, that is, crumbs or specks. This is the primary reason why the early Church moved to Communion on the tongue.

The traditional Roman Rite contains layers of rubrics to avoid the dispersion of crumbs and stray droplets; the cleaning of vessels … the theology of fragments later.

There is scriptural support:

> *Open thy mouth, and eat what I give thee.* Ezekiel 2:8
> *Open thy mouth wide, and I will fill it.* Psalm 80:10

Who is the "I"?
Of course it is the Lord,
and the Lord alone may feed us!

This is the deepest reason why in the divine liturgy the Holy Sacrifice of the Mass, it must be the ordained minister who is acting in *persona Christi* on behalf of Christ distributes the Bread of Angels to the communicants (Chapter 9). This mode of receiving – in the East and West – symbolizes and emphasizes several truths at once (Kwasniewski): [15]

1. The one doing the feeding is Christ.
   I do not feed myself.

2. *I am incapable of nourishing myself supernaturally; I must be fed, like a little child.*

Once I reach the threshold of divinity, it is imperative that I demonstrate to myself and in the site of others that at this threshold, I must kneel or take a passive stand to allow myself to be acted upon.

I am not there to feed myself as an autonomous agent, or to collect something that can add to my personal life portfolio. I am imposed upon and altered. The divine food is more powerful than I am, and I submit to it.

3. I am not the one who determines the conditions or the timing on the watch, Christ will act on me. By coming forward and submitting to the hand of another, I relinquish my mastery. There is no moment between reception and eating; to receive is to eat.

4. *More particularly we wait for Lord. Blessed are those servants whom the Lord, when he comes, shall find watching.*

And if on a communion rail, or a series of kneelers aligned in front which some parishes have done, the priest is the one who moves from communicant to communicant, while we remain steady on our knees, waiting for that anointed hand to bestow its blessing to the communicant, kneeling at the altar rail, waiting for God to come to him, as the priest makes his rounds – he's being the primary agent, as God is; he then gives us the food at the proper time.

5. *There is a clear hierarchy of distinction between the one giving the divine gift and the one receiving it.*

Because the communicant kneels down at an altar rail or kneeler while the priest or deacon remains standing, there is a strong differentiation of persons and actions. The relationship is reminiscent of the dove on the baptized. The conferral of the man "from above" imitates the descent of the son of God in His Incarnation, in order to lift us up to his heavenly glory.

Garrigou-Lagrange OP observes: *To debase ourselves before the most high is to recognize, not only in a speculative, but in a practical manner, our inferiority, littleness, and indignance, manifest in us, even though we are innocent, and, once we have sinned, it consists in recognizing our wretchedness.* [16]

From Kwasniewski:[17]

Therefore, against this millennial tradition, the abrupt return of Communion in the hand in the 1960s sent one and only one signal: the Eucharist and the priest aren't such a big deal after all. Don't worry about kneeling or bowing profoundly before it; don't worry about being fed with the Bread of Angels. It's just a symbol of our communal belonging and how great we already are by our baptism.

We see that one consistent set of symbols – developed overtime by the Church that, guided by the Holy Spirit, believed, profoundly in transubstantiation, and the real presence – has been replaced by another set, contrary to it, erosive of these beliefs.

How hard is it to see that this change of liturgical practice on reception of Communion has eroded belief in the Real Presence and cannot have been caused by the same Spirit who established a millennial tradition of Communion kneeling and on the tongue.

Resources, Notes

1 Kwasniewski, *The Holy Bread of Eternal Life, Restoring Eucharistic Reverence in an age of Impiety* (Manchester, N.H: Sophia Institute Press, 2020), 111.
2 Source: New Advent: https://www.newadvent.org/fathers/310123.htm. Accessed August 20, 2024.
3 Kwasniewski, *The Holy Bread of Eternal Life,* 107,108. Michael Fiedrowicz and Athanasius Schneider,experts in patrology, suggest the "bow" was far more profound in ancient times as illustrated here, and not standing fully upright, the head bowing down to the hand.
4 Ibid., 97, 110.
5 Ibid., P 110-111.
6 Ibid., 109.
7 Ibid., P 107, 121.
8 Ibid., 106.
9 Ibid., 112, 123, Also See Alcuin Reid, O.S.B, *The Organic Development of the Liturgy* (San Francisco: Ignatius press) 35.
10 Kwasniewski, *The Holy Bread of Eternal Life,* 108, 115, 116.
11 Our Sunday Visitor, https://www.oursundayvisitor.com/is-it-the-norm-to-receive-communion-in-the-hand/ Accessed July 8,2025. Also see ETWN, https://www.ewtn.com/catholicism/library/objecting-to-communion-in-the-hand-4911. Accessed July 6, 2025.
12 Kwasniewski, *The Holy Bread of Eternal Life,* 117-119.
13 Ibid., 114.
14 Ibid., 98.
15 Ibid., 99-102.
16 Réginald Garrigou-Lagrange, O.P., on Humility in the Interior Life.
17 Kwasniewski, *The Holy Bread of Eternal Life*, 119, 120.

"Out of reverence towards this Sacrament, nothing touches it, but what is consecrated." **—St. Thomas Aquinas**

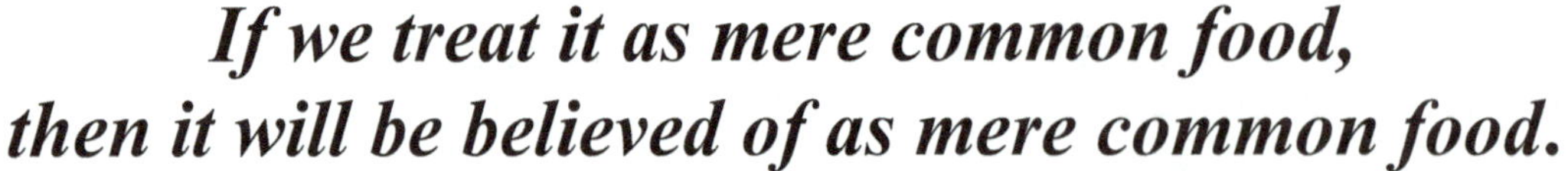

If we treat it as mere common food, then it will be believed of as mere common food.

DISCUSSION

The Right to Receive Communion in the Traditional Manner [1]

This seems to come up all the time: Catholics being denied or discouraged from receiving kneeling, and also on the tongue. While this was covered above, Canon Law specifies that Catholics have a right to receive in a traditional manner, that is, kneeling and on the tongue. ***This right cannot be denied.*** Receiving on the tongue is a practice with a long tradition and is seen as expressing reverence for the Eucharist. The indult did not eliminate on the tongue.

- **Right to Receive on the Tongue:**

Canon law protects the right of the faithful to receive Communion on the tongue. This right is not to be infringed upon …

"In distributing Holy Communion it is to be remembered that 'sacred ministers may not deny the sacraments to those who seek them in a reasonable manner, are rightly disposed, and are not prohibited by law from receiving them' (Code of Canon Law, can. 843 § 1; cf. can. 915). Hence any baptized Catholic who is not prevented by law must be admitted to Holy Communion. Therefore, it is not licit to deny Holy Communion to any of Christ's faithful solely on the grounds, for example, that the person wishes to receive the Eucharist kneeling or standing" (*Redemptionis Sacramentum*, no. 91).

- **Reverence and Tradition:**

Receiving on the tongue is seen as a way to express greater reverence for the Eucharist and to minimize the possibility of profaning the sacred species.

- **Pastoral Concerns:**

The practice of Communion in the hand was introduced in some regions due to pastoral concerns, but it is not simply a restoration of a historical practice.

- **Individual Choice:**

Ultimately, the choice of whether to receive on the tongue or in the hand is a personal one *for the communicant.*

- **Pastoral Prudence:**

While the right to receive on the tongue is protected, there may be situations where a priest or bishop, due to specific circumstances (like a pandemic), might temporarily restrict the practice.

1 There are numerous resources one can review. These four are helpful from the USCCB, EWTN, Catholic Answers, and *Crisis Magazine* (all accessed July 5, 2025) …
https://www.usccb.org/prayer-and-worship/the-mass/order-of-mass/liturgy-of-the-eucharist/the-reception-of-holy-communion-at-mass.
https://www.ewtn.com/catholicism/library/objecting-to-communion-in-the-hand-4911.
https://www.catholic.com/magazine/online-edition/how-ancient-is-communion-in-the-hand.
https://crisismagazine.com/opinion/when-communion-on-the-tongue-is-forbidden.

Ecclesial Documents

To reiterate what was covered above, the universal law of the Latin rite is that we receive Communion on the tongue. To receive in the hand is an indult or by special permission that does not exist in some parts of the world. ***By law, it is a right of the faithful to receive on the tongue, and the faithful must not have their rights denied.***

The Vatican has long promoted Communion on the tongue not only for its long tradition but because it "expresses the faithful's reverence for the Eucharist" and "removes the danger of profanation of the sacred species" (*Memorial Domini*).

Since the indult was granted, and as feared by Paul VI, profanation of the sacred species does occur, sacred hosts found in the pews, and thefts of Hosts for sacrilegious purposes. In 2005 there was an auction on eBay for what was presented as a Host consecrated by Pope St. John Paul II.

For this reason, it is important for the communicant to consume the Host <u>before</u> walking off to the side, not just so they are receiving with a paten to catch the fragments, but also to minimize any intentions to desecrate the sacred species.

Pope St. John Paul II:

In some countries the practice of receiving Communion in the hand has been introduced. This practice has been requested by individual episcopal conferences and has received approval from the Apostolic See. However, cases of a deplorable lack of respect toward the eucharistic species have been reported, cases that are imputable not only to the individuals guilty of such behavior but also to the pastors of the church who have not been vigilant enough regarding the attitude of the faithful toward the Eucharist. It also happens, on occasion, that the free choice of those who prefer to continue the practice of receiving the Eucharist on the tongue is not taken into account in those places where the distribution of Communion in the hand has been authorized. (*Dominicae Cenae* n. 11)

The GIRM

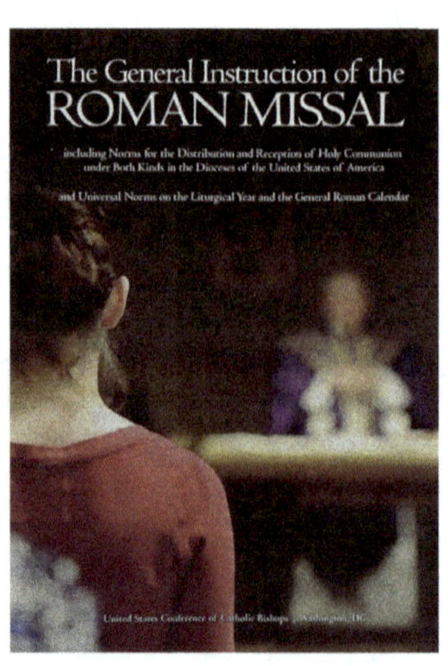

In its directives for distributing Communion:

The consecrated host may be received either on the tongue or in the hand, at the discretion of each communicant. . . . The priest raises the host slightly and shows it to each, saying, *Corpus Christi* (the Body of Christ). The communicant replies *Amen* and receives the sacrament either on the tongue or, where this is allowed and if the communicant so chooses, in the hand. (160–161). Notice that it says, "The consecrated host may be received either on the tongue or in the hand, at the discretion of each communicant." It does not say, "At the discretion of the extraordinary minister of the Eucharist" or "at the discretion of the priest or bishop."

ACTION POINTS

Dealing with the fragments .... What can we do now?

Until patens again become predominant in our parishes, or people start receiving Communion on the tongue, it's important that Catholics become aware of this problem. For those receiving in the hand, they need to be continually reminded to check for fragments in the hand and consume them using their tongue. Consume the Host in front of the priest. Perhaps having to continually remind people of this practice, in of itself, will prompt the easier solution of purchasing and using patens. Bad practices are habits that are hard to break. It is hoped that priests will also remind people prior to receiving Communion. This can be done in a charitable and discrete way. Perhaps it's your friend who attends Mass with you. Perhaps it's members of your family. We can no longer allow fragments of the sacred Host to be indiscriminately scattered across the floor, to be stepped on, to be vacuumed up, or scattered back into the pews where people return after Communion.

Brilliant!

A priest in Tyler Texas, while cleaning the post communion fragments from the sacred vessels at the altar, began a short discourse:

" I apologize for the time I am taking, but there are fragments up here that must be cleaned up because every fragment is in fact the Body, Blood Soul and divinity of Jesus Christ…"

He then proceeded to remind people receiving in the hand to also check for fragments.

A catechetical moment! There was a subliminal message as well.
Those that heard this message, not realizing this concern, may have well decided that it would be far better to just receive on the tongue. This priest may have well accomplished this without even specifically recommending the traditional manner of receiving Holy Communion.

Come up with your own "back-pocket" manner of instructing those that are at Mass with you! Pray …

I believe. I adore. I hope and I love thee. I ask pardon of you for those who do not believe, do not adore, do not hope, and do not love thee. Amen.

Notes

An Act of Faith in the Real Presence

Lord Jesus Christ, I believe you are truly present in this holy Sacrament, under the signs of bread and wine, as you were when dying upon the cross for the salvation of all, or as you are now enthroned in glory in heaven at the right hand of the Father.

You said that you would give yourself as the bread of life, which if we eat, we shall live forever. I believe this truth because you are truth itself. With confidence in your loving forgiveness therefore, I approach your altar, conscious that my unworthiness to receive you is outweighed by your desire to be united with my soul. You desire to nourish it on its earthly pilgrimage, until the day when I shall be with you in the eternal banquet, the feed on the unveiled beauty of your presence forever.

Amen.

Chapter 9 How Are We Fed?

Who is Administering the Eucharist

One of the issues identified in the survey conducted by the Real Presence Coalition that contributed to the loss and belief in the Real Presence, is the use of many extraordinary eucharistic ministers. This then, whether be standing or kneeling affects our reverence and the special nature of the Eucharist we're receiving.

Who should administer it? [1]

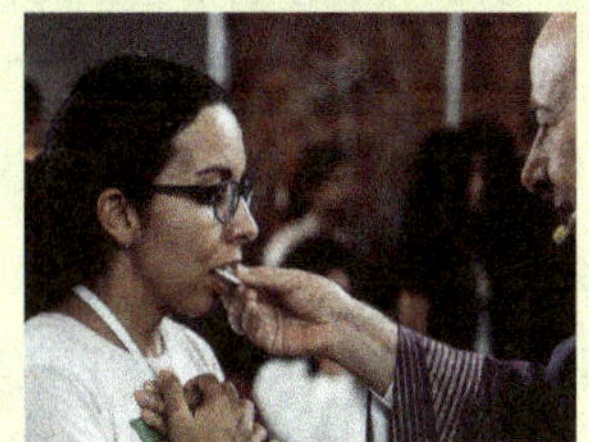

If you attend an ordination Mass, there is a point where the hands of the newly ordained priests are anointed – a rite that applies only to the priest. This goes back to the early Church. It is the priest's hands that will consecrate the bread and wine into the Body and Blood of Jesus Christ. The priest's hands are specially consecrated with holy oil so that he may fittingly *handle* the Blessed Sacrament, that he may touch and administer the holy gifts of the altar.

Pope St. John Paul II in *Dominicae Cenae.* n.11:

,,. one must not forget the primary office of priests, who have been consecrated by their ordination to represent Christ the Priest: for this reason their hands, like their words and their will, have become the direct instruments of Christ. Through this fact, that is, as ministers of the Holy Eucharist, they have a primary responsibility for the sacred species, because it is a total responsibility; they offer the bread and wine, they consecrate it, and then distribute the sacred species to the participants in the assembly who wish to receive them ...

How eloquent is the ancient custom …the rite of anointing of the hands in our Latin ordination, as though precisely for these hands, a special grace and power of the Holy Spirit is necessary! To touch the sacred species and to distribute them with their own hands was a privilege of the ordained, one which indicates an active participation in the ministry of the Eucharist.

A layman's hands in contrast are not anointed in this way. They do not represent Christ in the Mass, or serve as His direct instrument, or are responsible for His Body; or play an active part in eucharistic ministry. Kwasniewski:

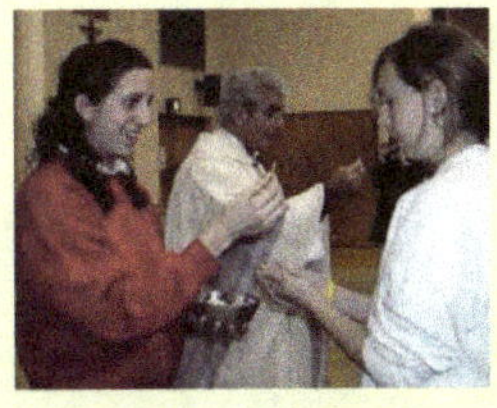

Does this not convey: I am grown up, and I can feed myself, thank you very much; the priest hands are no different, no better than mine." Maybe it's because the Eucharist isn't very special. Not really Christ?

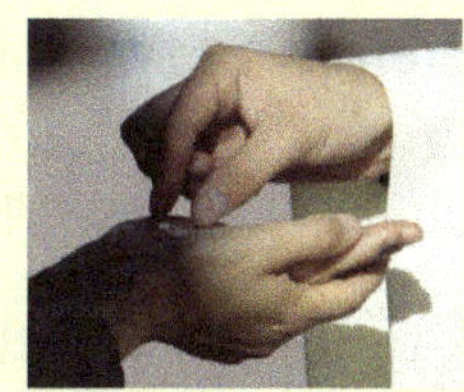

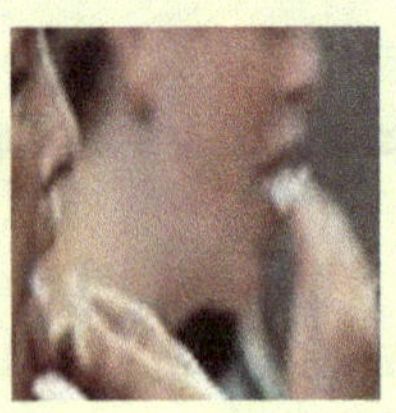

In short: [2]
We cannot feed ourselves. Only Christ the high priest gives us the Bread of Life, and his ordained minister in his place, set apart by Holy Orders, his hands likewise set apart for the task of a divine role, more fearful and inspiring than anything else that is done or could be done by us the children.

Kwasniewski: By flattening the divine into a human, to create and support the fatal atmosphere of the *egalitarianism* (we are all equal), *horizontalism and activism* that has poisoned the spiritual life of the Church for a half century. [3]

In fact, if the priest is the *alter Christus* (other Christ) has been set aside by a divine act of transformation to bring about Christ the high priest on the altar then we could only conclude, as Pope St. John Paul II stated, that the priest is also the one authorized by God to handle the most holy gifts and the distribute them to others, the fitting imparter of the Bread of Angels to the mouth of Christians. Instead. standing and receiving in the hand with people lined up in a queue, systematically undermines all of these symbolic aesthetic aspects of the act of Eucharistic Communion.[4]

By receiving the Host in the hand, more or less at high-level with the distributor, I become the one who feeds myself. I am now a grown up vis-à-vis God, with whom I relate to on my terms. I determine when I put this host into my mouth (or as in well documented cases, taken away for a souvenir, or put it in a hymnal, or used for a satanic ritual).[5]

Kwasniewski continues:
I assert my independence and control.
Communion in the hand, standing, means I come to Christ and his Church when and as it suits me, in my active, busy lifestyle.

Who gets to decide the conditions for Communion?

In the Catholic tradition, it is the feeder, i.e. the one giving the food, who decides the conditions for Communion; and this is not primarily the minister, or even the Church, but Christ himself!

No one would contend, of course, that these meanings are consciously intended by everyone who receives in the hand. *But these meanings are built into the action itself,* even as the opposite meanings are conveyed. Having many extraordinary ministers handing out the Host diminishes the idea of the sacredness and uniqueness of the Holy Eucharist. Yes, there is a shortage of priests, but how much time is really saved?

Again back to the objective. This all lends to the notion that the Eucharist isn't as special as it should be considered to be. It, like these other practices, erodes belief in the Real Presence.

THE SACRED VESSELS [6]

Adding to the previous discussion, and the earlier discussion of the importance of preventing any loss of fragments, current universal liturgical law states (GIRM 163, 270) that only priests, deacons, and formally instituted acolytes may handle sacred vessels, such as the chalice during the purification of sacred vessels after Communion capturing any fragments of the Host.

There has been a long standing practice going back to the Council of Trent that the vessels that are consecrated and that touched Christ are never touched by the laity. The Catechism of the Council of Trent, the magisterium's first universal catechism, published in 1566 as a witness to the faith, explains this point with irrefutable logic.[7]

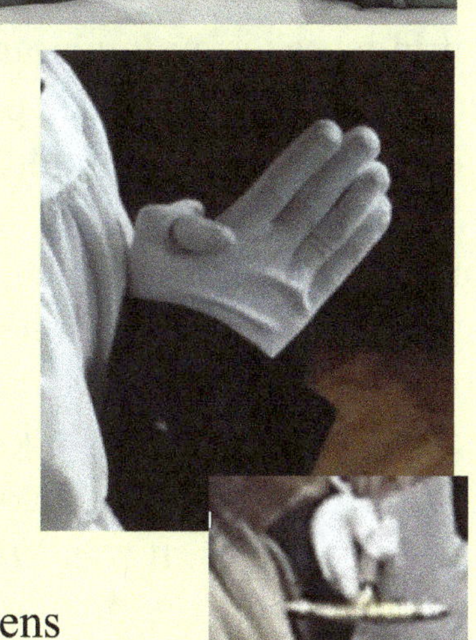

This practice also sent a message … supporting the very special nature of the Eucharist to the point where even the vessels that contain the Eucharist are *special.*

"Out of reverence towards this Sacrament, nothing touches it, but what is consecrated."
— St. Thomas Aquinas

Another *optic* !!

In an attempt to reclaim this traditional practice, some parishes now have the servers and sacristans handling the patens wearing white gloves or cloth if they need to move the sacred vessels.

Resources, Notes

1 Peter Kwasniewski, *The Holy Bread of Eternal Life, Restoring Eucharistic Reverence in an age of Impiety* (Manchester, N.H: Sophia Institute Press, 2020). 95-99.
2 Ibid., 99-103.
3 Ibid., 96.
4 Ibid., 95, 98.
5 Ibid., 99-103.
6 Ibid., P 96-97, fn. 100, 97. Also see the prior 1917 Code of Cannon Law, n. 1306.
7. Also see the 1917 Code of Cannon Law, n. 1306.

DISCUSSION

Moving toward what is *appropriate*

In as much as the priest alone can act in *persona Christi capitis* in the person of Christ, the Head of the Church, his ordination has set him apart essentially, not accidentally, for that office, and for all activities that flow from it. Therefore, it is fitting for him to feed himself and then to feed the other members of the church as Christ did to his Apostles at the last Supper.

Because of the indult, a concession granted from what was considered a liturgical abuse, it is currently ***acceptable*** to receive Communion standing and in the hand.

We need to move from what is *acceptable* towards what is ***appropriate***, to what is ***fitting.*** It is ***fitting*** that we assume this posture and mode of receiving of Holy Communion.

Fitting and appropriate are two terms commonly used not only in Catholic practice, but also theologically as well. The two terms by definition (Oxford) can be used synonymously:
Appropriate: suitable or proper in the circumstances.
Fitting: suitable or appropriate under the circumstances; right or proper.

"Fittingness" is an important term that has theological implications found in many ecclesial documents, even dogmatic proclamations. For example, *Munificentissimus Deus,* by Pope Pius XII on the Assumption of Mary. Paragraph 21:

"Thus St. John Damascene, an outstanding herald of this traditional truth, spoke out with powerful eloquence when he compared the bodily Assumption of the loving Mother of God with her other prerogatives and privileges. "It was ***fitting*** that she, who had kept her virginity intact in childbirth, should keep her own body free from all corruption even after death. It was ***fitting*** that she, who had carried the Creator as a child at her breast, should dwell in the divine tabernacles. It was ***fitting*** that the spouse, whom the Father had taken to himself, should live in the divine mansions. It was ***fitting*** that she, who had seen her Son upon the cross and who had thereby received into her heart the sword of sorrow which she had escaped in the act of giving birth to him, should look upon him as he sits with the Father. It was ***fitting*** that God's Mother should possess what belongs to her Son, and that she should be honored by every creature as the Mother and as the handmaid of God."

So it was *fitting* for Mary to be assumed into heaven.
AND
it is also *fitting* that we return to Communion kneeling and on the tongue, if we are ever going to regain proper reverence and reverse the current trend of the loss of belief in the Real Presence.

ACTION POINTS

The use of white gloves for the servers is a useful practice, not only for the optics which conveys not only the special nature of what is being handled during Mass, but also gives a unique aspect to the vessels; again, the optics.

Can this be expanded to other practices, such as servers distributing the consecrated wine?

To discuss:

Comment from a priest:

Europe and America do not realize how much damage they have done to the Church and other places because of their progressivism and egoism. Most rural churches elsewhere [in the world] are still following the traditional reception of the Eucharist on the tongue while kneeling. That was how the missionaries taught them. The missionaries represented the Church in Europe and America, but like every tradition handed down by Europe and America, they flip it on the rest of the world the moment the rest of the world is about to catch up and felt comfortable with anything Europe and America had brought. The damage of this is enormous, especially creating a lack of trust and doubt of everything Europe and America has provided with Christianity getting hardest hit of all.

Notes

Prayer of Saint Bonaventure

Pierce, O most sweet Lord Jesus, my inmost soul with the most joyous and healthful wound of Thy love, and with true, calm and most holy apostolic charity, that my soul may ever languish and melt with entire love and longing for Thee, may yearn for Thee and for thy courts, may long to be dissolved and to be with Thee.

Grant that my soul may hunger after Thee, the Bread of Angels, the refreshment of holy souls, our daily and super substantial bread, having all sweetness and savor and every delightful taste.

May my heart ever hunger after and feed upon Thee, Whom the angels desire to look upon, and may my inmost soul be filled with the sweetness of Thy savor; may it ever thirst for Thee, the fountain of life, the fountain of wisdom and knowledge, the fountain of eternal light, the torrent of pleasure, the fullness of the house of God; may it ever compass Thee, seek Thee, find Thee, run to Thee, come up to Thee, meditate on Thee, speak of Thee, and do all for the praise and glory of Thy name, with humility and discretion, with love and delight, with ease and affection, with perseverance to the end; and be Thou alone, ever my hope, my entire confidence, my riches, my delight, my pleasure, my joy, my rest and tranquility, my peace, my sweetness, my food, my refreshment, my refuge, my help, my wisdom, my portion, my possession, my treasure; in Whom may my mind and my heart be ever fixed and firm and rooted immovably. Amen.

Chapter 10 Toward A Near Term Solution

In Reflection …

Belief in the Real presence is rapidly eroding, even among those who still attend Mass.

From *Memoriale Domini*: *... the new mode (in the hand) "should not suggest to him (the layperson) that this is ordinary bread, or just any sacred object... This respectful attitude should be proportionate to what he is doing* [emphasis added, Appendix, p.107].

Kwasniewski:[1] "It is impossible to reread this optimistic language from fifty years ago, without saying that these conditions were never met, are still not being met, and in fact will never be *able* to be met" if we ignore the problem. They are habitually violated. We need greater reverence when we are in the presence of the Lord. And how much more of this is true when we receive Him in Holy Communion.

As a *continuing* eucharistic revival and reform …the hope is to curtail Communion in the hand and gradually replace it soon with the *normative* traditional practice. It will take time.

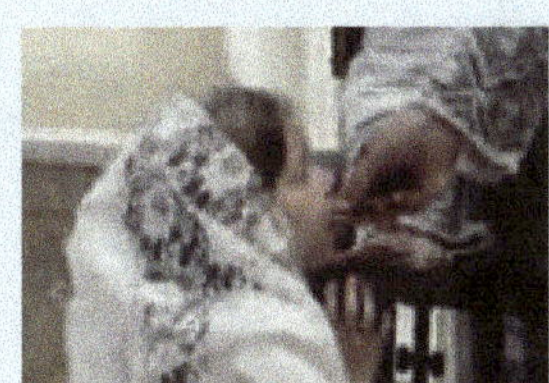

There is an urgent need to recover a reverent manner of distributing and receiving Holy Communion as encouraged by Pope Benedict XVI one of several strong proponents of reception on the tongue by the faithful who are kneeling.

Besides Pope Benedict, Cardinal Sarah, Bishop Schneider, and many others clergy are *pleading* for the restoration of a traditional practice that emerged out of and reinforces the Catholic faith. *When will other church leaders pay heed?*

Kwasniewski continues: One has to hope that this dire situation cannot last forever. "There will always be clergy who will see clearly their solemn duties before God and man, and will take these duties seriously. Meanwhile, we must keep up our prayer life in all the ways that are open to us and all the faithful. In this way, we will be strengthened for the journey through the desert."

"At the same time, we do not live anymore in the 4th century; we live in the 21st, after a millennium (and more) during which the Church moved by the Holy Spirit, abandoned Communion in the hand everywhere because of ever-growing reverence for the most Holy Sacrament, a deepening appreciation of the special anointing conferred on the hands of the priest for handling sacred things, and a realization of the dangers connected with hand reception."

"Something that might have been acceptable in one time period comes to be seen as unacceptable in another. Precisely because the Church practices changed, as her insight into repealed mysteries developed. One who interprets this late development as a corruption has essentially espoused Protestantism or its close relative, false *antiquarianism"*

It is the hope that every lay person can make a firm commitment, for the glory of God and the sanctification of their souls, always to receive our Lord kneeling, and on the tongue, at every Mass they attend, anywhere, at any time.

In general, once we all become aware of the problem surrounding Communion in the hand – that allows for easy and repeated profanation, and has *contributed to the loss of faith in the Real Presence* and the special nature of the ordained priesthood, that contradicts fitting tradition of many centuries; and, the practice is contrary, even to the stipulations that are supposed to be regulated, that it facilitates the theft of the Host for satanic rituals, etc. – priests and extraordinary Eucharistic ministers must be very vigilant in the distribution of communion in the hand.

Where do we begin?

We begin with prayer. From here, we gather with other friends and family from our parish and, when the time is right, meet with the parish staff, and of course the pastor. Bring your concerns to him. And then offer some steps to move in a different direction. Start small. Gradualism is the key. Be reasonable. For example, don't propose altar rails when the parish architecture or budget will not accommodate them.
With these considerations, below is as a list of tasks to be performed.

USE OF PATENS and GLOVES

It has already been noted in Chapter 6, when Communion standing and in the hand was implemented in the early 1970s, the paten began to fall in disuse during Communion. In as much as Communion in the hand significantly results in the fragments falling on the floor and elsewhere, it is critical that the paten again be reinstated at all parishes. *This is actually the most serious problem that needs to be corrected.* The pastor should *frequently remind* communicants to consume the Host directly in front of the priest, not to one side, and remind those who are receiving in hand to check and consume any fragments. Bad habits take time to correct. You've now provided a subtle encouragement that Communion in the hands is not a good idea. This sets the stage for the use of the paten. When introduced, explain *why* it is needed. Perhaps an article in the church bulletin will help. It's because of the fragments.

Some parishes already use a paten. Great! Average cost is about $70 each, although most parishes do have 1 or 2 available. The usual excuses for not using them …
This brings us back to the days of pre-Vatican II
We will have to train servers
It will cause confusion, disunity, and disruption.

Yes. **Care of the Eucharist does take effort.** We frequently take a pragmatic view of the Eucharist these days …we believe in the Real Presence, but not if it costs too much time or effort to implement.

The use of gloves was noted in chapter 9 as a means of avoiding handling of the sacred vessels. It also sends a visible sign. The Eucharist is so special that even the vessels that contain the sacred Hosts are special.

Training of servers is not a difficult task. Most parishes train young boys as young as seven years old. It is an excellent way to get young boys to serve. Each server's gloves can be kept in a marked Ziploc bag. White gloves can be ordered from pall bearer and safety supply companies in all sizes. They run about $2.50 a pair and can be a great KOC gift to the pastor!

Altar Rails and Kneelers

One of the most recent encouraging signs is the rise in the number of parishes installing altar rails. If you're in a parish with an existing altar rail, it's a no-brainer. Parishes with two or less steps up in front, rails will work with the communicant kneeling on the first step. But some parishes have three or four steps. This is a little more difficult.

The most convenient and cost-effective way of enabling those receiving Communion the opportunity to kneel is the use of the portable kneelers. Some can mount on the steps. Parishes typically have two to support a wedding. Kneelers provide support in getting up. A line of kneelers set up in front are more convenient for distributing Communion in so far as Communion takes less time. Extra wide kneelers placed together work well.

Option One

Most parishes using one or two person kneelers will typically set up two in front for the center aisle. Even in large parishes, people flow across the pews to the center aisle and then forward. Kneeler placement options, especially with more complicated pew arrangements, are provided in the **Appendix**. Prices vary dependent on kneeler design.

Option Two

Option Three

There is yet a third option when you do not have portable kneelers or an altar rail. Some parishes have elected to leave the front pew vacant during Mass. Communicants proceed down the center aisle and fill into that front row pew that functions as an altar rail. After Communion, the kneeler is raised, communicants depart with the next group filing in behind them.

Option Four

Altar rails are experiencing a resurgence as more of the laity desire to seek greater reverence during reception of Communion. Installing them involves various considerations such as choice of materials, dimensions, and how well they fit into existing church architecture. How they are secured to the church floor and that they are level and stable requires proper measurement and materials. Costs can reach $50,000, but less when designed as movable. However, feedback from parishes that have installed them has been very positive as covered in a 2025 article in the NCR which noted: [2]

"… the documents of Vatican II and the General Instruction of the Roman Missal do not call for the removal of altar rails. But since people could receive Communion standing up, in a misguided and imprudent move, the altar rails became part of the sacred architecture that was done away in many churches and left out of new ones being built — all to fit mistakenly into what was regarded as renovations for the reform of the times."

And …

"It is beautiful for me how people can come to the altar rail, how it's been seen as the extension of the altar called, sometimes, 'the people's altar.' It's that threshold between heaven and earth, heaven being the sanctuary and earth being the nave where the people are gathered," the rector said. "It's a beautiful symbol of the priest, the spiritual father, representing Christ, reaching from heaven over the threshold of that altar rail to give Communion to the spiritual children." … In addition to reverence, it's an efficient way of distributing Communion [with] no need for extraordinary ministers of Holy Communion." Fr. David Kwiatkowski, St. Anne Church in Richmond Hill, Georgia.

Bottom line is: options are available to provide a means for people to kneel (if able) or stand during Communion as was noted in the NCR article.

Resources, Notes

1 Peter Kwasniewski, *The Holy Bread of Eternal Life, Restoring Eucharistic Reverence in an age of Impiety* (Manchester, N.H: Sophia Institute Press, 2020). 122, 125.

2 *National Catholic Register*: https://www.ncregister.com/features/the-return-of-altar-rails Accessed July 6, 2025.

Appendix

I think that many people do not fully understand
the value of Mass,
because if they recognized
the enormous blessing we have in a Lord
who gives himself as our food and drink
in the Sacred Host,
they would go to Mass every day
to participate in the fruits of the sacrifice
and let go of so many superfluous things.

– St. Carlo Acutis

Chapter 1

This outline by Dr. Brant Pitre should assist one in teaching more on the Old Testament foreshadowing of the Eucharist ...

Jesus and the Jewish Roots of the Eucharist

Dr. Brant Pitre

The New Exodus

First Exodus	New Exodus
1. Deliverer: Moses	1. New Deliverer: Messiah
2. Israel: Released from Egypt	2. Israel and Gentiles: Released from the Sin, Exile, and Death
3. Journey to Promised Land	3. Journey: New Promised Land (New Eden)
4. Worship of God: Tabernacle/Temple	4. Worship of God: New Temple
5. Ultimate Destination: Jerusalem	5. Ultimate Destination: New Jerusalem

New Passover

1. In order to have a New Exodus, you must first have a New Passover
2. Old Testament Passover: (Exodus 12)
    a. Father was priest over his family (cf. Exodus 24)
    b. Unblemished Male Lamb taken and sacrificed; blood poured into bowl
    c. Dip hyssop branch in blood
    d. Spread blood on the doorposts of the home
    e. Eat the Lamb
3. Later Jewish Passover
    a. Passover Night: Child would ask the Father:
    b. "Why is this night different from other nights?"
    c. "Why do we eat unleavened bread and roast lamb?"
    d. Father's Answer: "It is because of what the LORD did for *me* when I came out of Egypt" (Exodus 13:8)
3. Passover Liturgy: spiritually *brought them back* to *participate* in First Passover:
    "In every generation a man must so regard himself as if he came forth himself out of Egypt, for it is written... [Exod 13:8]. Therefore we are bound to give thanks...." (Mishnah *Pesahim* 10)

4. Jesus' New Passover:
    a. The Last Supper: What is different? (Mark 14; Matt 24; Luke 22)
        1. No mention of the Lamb (cf. Exodus 32)
        2. Jesus speaks of "pouring out" blood; only priests can do this (Lev 4:5-7)
    b. The New Passover:
        1. New Priests: Jesus and 12 Apostles (representing 12 Tribes)
        2. New Lamb: Jesus replaces Lamb with himself
        3. New Sacrifice: Unleavened Bread (Body) and Wine (Blood) offered

4. Why did Jewish Christians believe Eucharist was Jesus' body and blood?
    a. Eucharist, like the Old Passover: is a *participation* in the New Passover of Jesus
    b. You had to *eat* the Lamb to complete the sacrifice
    c. St. Paul: Jesus is the New Lamb
    "Christ, our paschal lamb, has been sacrificed. Therefore let us keep the feast!" (1 Cor 5:7-8)

New Manna

1. If Jesus inaugurates a New Exodus, what food is given for the journey?

Jesus and the Jewish Roots of the Eucharist
Dr. Brant Pitre

2. Old Testament Manna:
    a. The Manna in the Wilderness (Exodus 16)
        1. Israel cries out for food; they want to go back to Egypt
        2. The LORD says: "Behold, I will rain down bread from heaven for you"
        3. In the Morning: "Bread" from heaven (Manna)
        4. In the Evening: "Flesh" from heaven (Quail)
        5. Manna: white, tasted "like wafers made with honey"
            (A foretaste of the promised land: "milk and honey")
        6. "The Grain of Heaven" and "The Bread of Angels" (Psa 78:21-25)
    b. The Manna in the Tabernacle:
        1. Placed in a Golden Urn perpetually "before the LORD" in the Ark
            (Exod 16:33-34; Heb 9:6)

3. Jesus and the New Manna:
    a. The Lord's Prayer: "Give us this day our daily bread" (Matt 6:11; Luke 11:3)
        1. What kind of bread?
            a. Daily: "Each day"
            b. Supernatural: "Give us this day our *epi-ousios* bread"
                1.Greek: *epi* ("on, upon, above")
                ousios ("substance, being, nature")
            c. St. Jerome: "Give us this day our *supersubstantial* bread"
            c. Both daily *and* supernatural: just like the Manna
        2. "Taken literally, (*epiousious* – "superessential")... refers directly to the
            Bread of Life, the Body of Christ" (CCC 2837)

    b. The Bread of Life Discourse (John 6: 48-64)

Jesus said: "I am the bread of life. *Your fathers ate the manna in the wilderness, and they died.* This is the bread which comes down from heaven, that a man might eat of it and not die. I am the living bread which came down from heaven; if any one eats of this bread, he will live for ever; and *the bread which I shall give for the life of the world is my flesh.*"The Jews then disputed among themselves, saying, "How can this man give us his flesh to eat?" So Jesus said to them, "Amen, amen, I say to you, unless you eat the flesh of the Son of Man and drink his blood, you have no life in you; he who eats my flesh and drinks my blood has eternal life, *and I will raise him up at the last day.* For my flesh is true food, and my blood is true drink.... *This is the bread which comes down from heaven, not such as the fathers ate and died*; he who eats this bread will live forever." Many of his disciples, when they heard it, said, "This is a hard saying; who can listen to it?" But Jesus, knowing in himself that his disciples murmured at it, said to them, "Do you take offense at this? *Then what if you were to see the Son of Man ascending where he was before*? It is the spirit that gives life, the flesh is of no avail; the words that I have spoken to you are spirit and life. But there are some of you that do not believe"

4. Why did Jewish Christians believe the Eucharist was Jesus' body and blood?
    a. They knew it is *supernatural* bread *from heaven*
    b. They knew it is his *risen* body and blood

New "Bread of the Presence"

1. Worship of God in First Exodus: Tabernacle
2. Old Testament "Bread of the Presence" (Commonly mis-translated "Showbread")
    a. God Instructs Moses to Build the Tabernacle (Exodus 25:10-40)

Chapter 3

Regarding Dress Code

Imagine if the bishop or priest celebrating Mass came out wearing shorts, tank top, and flip-flops! Most people would be shocked and would not hesitate to voice their objections. So why does there seem to be a different standard for the laity attending Mass? Yes, the celebrant is ordained to the ministerial priesthood, but all baptized belong to the common priesthood of the Christian faithful. Both the clergy and the laity come to offer sacrifice at Holy Mass and receive our Lord in Holy Communion. The clergy have prescribed investments, but the laity should also show respect for God in His house of worship by dressing appropriately with proper reverence, not as if they're going to the beach or a picnic. Most of our churches are air-conditioned, so summertime heat should not be an excuse. Even if the church is not air-conditioned, A person can wear cooler clothing while still being dressed modestly.

The catechism of the Catholic Church has this to say about dressing properly for Mass: "To prepare for worthy reception of this sacrament [i.e. the Eucharist], the faithful should observe the fast required in their Church. Bodily demeanor (gestures, clothing) ought to convey the respect, solemnity, and joy of this moment when Christ becomes our guest" (CCC 1387)." What does dressing "modestly" or "properly" or "appropriately" mean in practice?

There is a dress code for St. Peters Basilica in Rome that must be followed by all visitors, irrespective of age or gender, so we can look at their dress code for guidance. According to their website, A guide to the St. Peter Basilica Dress Code, "Roman Catholic Churches have always had a dress code dating back to the earliest centuries. Doing Mass at St. Peters Basilica, men and women are required to cover their knees and shoulders. Men can wear trousers and shirts, while women can wear long skirts or dresses, both of which must cover the knees. Women are allowed to wear hats for Mass, however, men must take their hats off before entering the church. The following are listed under "What to wear to St. Peter's Basilica": shirts or blouses that cover your shoulders: plain T-shirts, formal shirts, or full sleeved blouses, or tops are permitted. Trousers or skirts that cover your knees: pants to cover your knees and long skirts or dresses can be worn inside the Basilica. The following are listed under "What not to wear to St. Peter's Basilica": sleeveless shirts or tops: avoid wearing anything sleeveless or with straps or anything too tight. Low cut tops: low cut tops or crop tops that expose your chest or stomach are strictly forbidden. Shorts or skirts that are above the knee: Do not wear mini skirts or shorts that don't cover your knees. Obscene or offensive tattoos: if you have any offensive tattoos, make sure you cover them up before you head into the Church.

The above should be considered minimum standards. Of course, people may voluntarily choose to dress even more formally if they wish. For example, it would be a great sign of respect for a man to wear a suit and tie in church. Some women choose to follow the traditional custom of wearing a head covering such as a Mantilla or a lace or silk liturgical veil.

We have just completed our three year National Eucharistic Revival, intending to promote a greater understanding and respect for the Real Presence of Christ in the Eucharist. Dressing properly for the Holy Sacrifice of the Mass is a great way to express in a concrete and practical way that we do believe that Jesus Christ is really present at Mass and show our love and esteem for our Lord and Savior as he comes into our hearts during Holy Communion. May God give us this grace Amen.

Most Reverend Thomas John Paprocki
Bishop, Diocese of Springfield
5 July 2025

Ref: https://www.youtube.com/watch?v=SLv7uuyfpY0. Accessed July 7, 2020.

Chapter 5
Genuflection 101

The Catholic Hour Author: Leon Suprenant | Posted: 26. March 2010 09:58

A few weeks ago someone posed this question to me:

I know we are always to genuflect when entering and leaving the church for Mass, but are we supposed to genuflect when coming for non-Masses, such as parent meetings for Confirmation?

This is a very good question for all of us to consider, even if we automatically genuflect whenever we enter a church could mean a virtue, a godly habit, but it could also mean a mindless act that we do without considering why we do it. So, let's look at this issue a little more closely.

Genuflection is the bending of the right knee to the floor and then rising again to a standing position as an act of reverence toward Our Lord, who is truly present, Body, Blood, Soul, and Divinity, in the most Blessed Sacrament. As St. Paul wrote, even at the name of Jesus, every knee must bend (Phil. 2:10). Even more, we should bend the knee before the Lord Himself!

We genuflect upon entering a church not strictly because it's a church building, but because Our Lord is present there in the tabernacle. Typically the tabernacle is in the center of the church, or in some other prominent place indicated by a sanctuary lamp that is kept burning. It is to this Presence that we genuflect.

A couple points. Obviously we reverence the Eucharist during Mass. You will notice, for example, that the priest genuflects immediately after the bread and wine are consecrated, as he acknowledges that Our Lord is now present on the altar.

Christ's presence in the Eucharist doesn't end when Mass is over. Hosts remaining after Mass are kept in the tabernacle, both for adoration of Our Lord outside of Mass, and also to give to the sick and dying as needed. Sometimes a large host is exposed in a monstrance for adoration, but even when the Eucharist is simply reserved in the tabernacle we should adore Him there, and one way we do that is by genuflecting when we come into His presence.

It follows, then, that we would genuflect upon entering the presence of the Lord when we walk into a church, regardless of whether we're there for Mass, for private prayer before Our Lord, or for some other parish event.

The only exception to that would be in the unusual case of the Blessed Sacrament not being reserved in the church. For example, sometimes the Sacrament is removed when the church is being cleaned or renovated, or when the church building is being used for a special (non-liturgical) event such as a concert.

And of course the tabernacle is empty on Good Friday, so next Friday one should simply bow to the altar. Whenever the Sacrament is not present in the tabernacle, the sanctuary lamp will not be burning.

Genuflecting may seem like a small thing, but this act of reverence is a building block that will lead to an ever more profound awareness of God's presence in our midst!

Should we make a sign of reverence entering the church?

Is making an act of reverence entering a Catholic Church *fitting* or *appropriate?*

A recommendation that it is *fitting* as a Catholic devotion takes precedence over an opinion that might suggest, for example, that the Rosary is merely repetitious prayer. As noted in Chapter 9 discussion, "fitting" has theological import as well and the term is used in ecclesial documents, such as the Dogma of Mary's Assumption. "Appropriate" can also fall into the category, but it is more often used in every day practices of Catholics.

Fr. Mike Schmitz

"The term reverence is traditionally attributed to an act or behavior affirming something perceived as divine and holy....Reverence expresses a call to recognize God in awe and wonder as evident in the book of Leviticus where we discover God's directive toward Israel to exercise moral holiness by keeping the sabbath and exercise *reverence toward God's sanctuary."* Leviticus, 19:30,

"Generally, **if the Blessed Sacrament is reserved in the church, it is customary to acknowledge the Lord's presence with a brief act of worship on entering or leaving the building** – normally, a genuflection in the direction of the place of reservation."

Marlon De La Torre, MA, MEd., PhD

"Generally, if the Blessed Sacrament is reserved in the church, it is customary to acknowledge the Lord's presence with a brief act of worship on entering or leaving the building – normally, a genuflection in the direction of the place of reservation."

Dr. Robert Fastiggi, Professor of Dogmatic Theology and Christology, Sacred Heart Major Seminary, Detroit.

"Reverence towards God is not an option. It is required by the virtue of religion, which includes the need to adore God and show Him reverence (cf. CCC 2096). I agree that it is certainly most appropriate to bless ourselves with holy water upon entering the Church. If we neglect to do this, it's not a sin. If, however, we enter a Church and fail to manifest reverence to the presence of God, the Incarnate Word, present in the Blessed Sacrament, then sin may be involved. I say "may" because some people, because of bad catechetical instruction, might not be fully culpable for their lack of reverence. Objectively speaking, though, **it is sinful to enter a Church and fail to show reverence to the presence of God.**"

Catholic Herald Diocese of Superior (Sept. 16 2022)

" ... This adoration of the Eucharist can be expressed through many different kinds of reverence. One simple way that we can bear witness to our belief in the real presence is simply by making the sign of the cross whenever we drive past a Catholic church. This act acknowledges Christ's presence in the Eucharist hosts that are reposed in the tabernacle. Similarly, **we genuflect upon entering a Catholic church** both in order to remind ourselves by a physical gesture that our Lord and God is present in the tabernacle, and to pay him homage."   Ref: "Reviving Reverence for the Eucharist" Aiden Jones

Diocese of Kansas City. Leon Suprenant and the Chancery Staff

"We genuflect **upon entering a church** not strictly because it's a church building, but because Our Lord is present there in the tabernacle."

Our Sunday Visitor

Mar 23, 2016 — *Touch your knee to the floor in reverence. Genuflect toward the tabernacle when you first enter the Church, your pew, and when you leave.*

Catholics are asked to show reverence and adoration whenever passing in front of the tabernacle, where the Eucharist is reserved. This is typically done by genuflecting, although if unable, a profound bow from the waist is acceptable. Be purposeful. Touch your knee to the floor in reverence. **Genuflect toward the tabernacle when you first enter the Church/your pew and when you leave.** If it's too hard physically, try to express reverence in some other way. When the Eucharist is exposed — that is, not inside the closed tabernacle — you should also genuflect.
https://www.oursundayvisitor.com/the-unofficial-newcomers-guide-to-the-church/

Cardinal Arinze

It is right that we should focus our reflection on reverence due to the Holy Eucharist. Many people have sadly noticed that in our churches there is a worrying **decline in reverence.** The matter is of great importance because of the central place of the Eucharistic Ministry in Catholic faith and life.

It is a beautiful practice that people who are near a church or chapel where the august Sacrament is reserved should pay visits to Our Lord, short or long as the case may be. There is also the praiseworthy habit of making the sign of the cross or bowing when one **drives past such a sacred place.**

Comment: If it is fitting and praiseworthy in making the sign of the cross when one drives past such a sacred place, as Cardinal Arinze states, how much more fitting is it to make the sign of the Cross or bow when entering?

Adoremus Dec 2013. Online Edition – Vol. IX, No. 9: December 2003 – January 2004. Cardinal Arinze: The Reverence due to the Holy Eucharist

Chapter 6

Memoriale Domini, the Instruction on the Manner of Administering Holy Communion

The Congregation for Divine Worship on May 29, 1969

When it celebrates the memorial of the Lord, by that rite the Church witnesses to its faith and adoration of Christ, who is present in the sacrifice and who is given as food to those who share in the Eucharistic table.

For this reason it is of great concern that the Eucharist be celebrated and shared in most worthily and fruitfully, by observing unchanged the tradition that has reached us step by step, the tradition whose riches have been poured into the practice and life of the Church. The documents of history demonstrate that the ways of celebrating and receiving the holy Eucharist have been diverse. Even in our time many and important ritual changes have been introduced into the celebration of the Eucharist in order to bring it into accord with the spiritual and psychological needs of men today. Because of circumstances, communion under both kinds, bread and wine, which was once common in the Latin rite but had fallen into disuse little by little, has again been made a part of the discipline governing the faithful's mode of receiving the holy Sacrament. At the time of the Council of Trent a different situation had arisen and was in effect everywhere; the Council approved and defended it as suited to the conditions of that period. (1)

With the renewal of the modes of communicating, however, the sign of the Eucharistic meal and the complete fulfillment of Christ's mandate have been effected more clearly and vividly. At the same time a full sharing in the celebration of the Eucharist, expressed through Sacramental communion, has recently stirred up in some places the desire to return to the practice by which the Eucharistic bread is placed in the hand of the faithful who communicates himself by putting it in his mouth.

In some communities and localities this rite has even been performed without obtaining the prior approval of the Apostolic See and occasionally without appropriate preparation for the people.

It is true that, according to ancient usage, it was once permitted for the faithful to take the sacred food in their hands and themselves to place it in their mouths and even, in the earliest period, to carry the holy Sacrament with them from the place of celebration, especially in order to receive it as viaticum if they should have to suffer for the profession of the faith.

Nevertheless the precepts of the Church and the writings of the Fathers give abundant witness to the great reverence and prudence shown to the holy Eucharist. For "no one . . . eats this flesh unless first he adores," (2) and each recipient is warned: ". . . receive it and take care that none of it be lost to you" (3): "for it is the body of Christ." (4)

In the meantime the care and ministry of the Body and Blood of the Lord was entrusted in a quite special way to sacred ministers or to persons assigned to this function: "After the president has completed the prayers and all the people have made the acclamation, those among us whom we call deacons distribute a part of the bread and wine and water, in which the thanksgiving has been made, to each one present and bring them to those who are absent." (5)

The office of bringing the Eucharist to those who were absent was soon entrusted to sacred ministers alone, for the reason that greater care might be shown for the reverence due to the Body of Christ as well as for the needs of the people. In the following period, after the true meaning of the Eucharistic mystery, its effect, and the presence of Christ in it had been profoundly investigated, from a pressing sense of reverence toward this holy Sacrament and of the humility which its reception demands, the custom was introduced by which the minister himself would place the piece of consecrated bread on the tongue of the communicants.

In view of the state of the Church as a whole today, this manner of distributing Holy Communion must be observed, not only because it rests upon a tradition of many centuries but especially because it is a sign of the reverence of the faithful toward the Eucharist. The practice in no way detracts from the personal dignity of those who approach this great Sacrament and it is a part of the preparation needed for the most fruitful reception of the Lord's body. (6)

This reverence is a sign of communion not in "common bread and drink" (7) but in the Body and Blood of the Lord. By it "the people of God shares in the blessings of the paschal sacrifice, renews the new covenant once made by God with man in the Blood of Christ, and in faith and hope prefigures and anticipates the eschatological banquet in the kingdom of the Father." (8)

In addition, this manner of communicating, which is now to be considered as prescribed by custom, gives more effective assurance that Holy Communion will be distributed with the appropriate reverence, decorum, and dignity; that any danger of profaning the Eucharistic species, in which "the whole and entire Christ, God and man, is substantially contained and permanently present in a unique way," (9) will be avoided; and finally that the diligent care which the Church has always commended for the very fragments of the consecrated bread will be maintained: "If you have allowed anything to be lost, consider this a lessening of your own members." (10)

On this account, since some few episcopal conferences and individual bishops had asked that the usage of placing the consecrated bread in the hand of the faithful be admitted in their territories, the Supreme Pontiff decreed that each bishop of the entire Latin Church should be asked his opinion concerning the appropriateness of introducing this rite. A change in a matter of such importance, which rests on a very ancient and venerable tradition, besides touching upon discipline can also include dangers. These may be feared from a new manner of administering Holy Communion: they are a lessening of reverence toward the noble Sacrament of the altar, its profanation, or the adulteration of correct doctrine

Three questions were therefore proposed to the bishops. Up to March 12 the following responses had been received:

1. Does it seem that the proposal should be accepted by which, besides the traditional mode, the rite of receiving Holy Communion in the hand would be permitted?

Yes: 567
No: 1,233
Yes, with reservations: 315
Invalid votes: 20

2. Should experiments with this new rite first take place in small communities, with the assent of the local Ordinary?

Yes: 751
No: 1,215
Invalid votes: 70

3. Do you think that the faithful, after a well planned catechetical preparation, would accept this new rite willingly?

Yes: 835
No: 1,185
Invalid votes: 128

From the responses received it is thus clear that by far the greater number of bishops feel that the present discipline should not be changed at all, indeed that if it were changed, this would be offensive to the sensibilities and spiritual appreciation of these bishops and of most of the faithful.

After he had considered the observations and the counsel of those whom "the Holy Spirit has placed as bishops to rule" (11) the Churches, in view of the seriousness of the matter and the importance of the arguments proposed, the Supreme Pontiff judged that the long received manner of ministering Holy Communion to the faithful should not be changed.

The Apostolic See therefore strongly urges bishops, priests, and people to observe zealously this law, valid and again confirmed, according to the judgment of the majority of the Catholic episcopate, in the form which the present rite of the sacred liturgy employs, and out of concern for the common good of the Church.

If the contrary usage, namely, of placing Holy Communion in the hand, has already developed in any place, in order to help the episcopal conference fulfill their pastoral office in today's often difficult situation, the Apostolic See entrusts to the conferences the duty and function of judging particular circumstances, if any. They may make this judgment provided that any danger is avoided of insufficient reverence or false opinions of the Holy Eucharist arising in the minds of the faithful and that any other improprieties be carefully removed.

In these cases, moreover, in order to govern this usage properly, the episcopal conferences should undertake the appropriate deliberations after prudent study; the decision is to be made by a two-thirds majority by secret ballot.

These deliberations should then be proposed to the Holy See for the necessary confirmation, together with an accurate explanation of the reasons which moved the conferences to take this action. The Holy See will weigh the individual cases with care, remembering the bonds which exist between the several local Churches among themselves and with the entire Church, in order to promote the common good and edification and the increase of faith and piety which flow from mutual good example.

This Instruction, prepared at the special mandate of the Supreme Pontiff Paul VI, was duly approved by him, in virtue of apostolic authority, on May 28, 1969. Pope Paul also decreed that it be brought to the attention of the bishops through the presidents of the episcopal conferences.

Anything to the contrary notwithstanding.

Rome, May 29, 1969.

Benno Card. Gut
Prefect

A. Bugnini
Secretary

FOOTNOTES:

1 Cf. Council of Trent, session XXI, doctrine concerning communion under both kinds and communion of children: Denz. 1726-1717 (930); session XXII, decree on the petition for the concession of the cup: Denz. 1760.

2 Augustine, *Enarrationes in Psalmos*, 98, 9: PL 37, 1264.

3 Cf. Cyril of Jerusalem, *Catecheses Mystagogicae*, V, 21: PG 33, 1126.

4 Hippolytus, *Traditio Apostolica*, n. 37; ed. B. Botte, 1963, p. 84.

5 Justin, *Apologia* I, 65: PG 6, 427.

6 Cf. Augustine, Enarrationes in Psalm os, 98, 9: PL 37, 1264-1265.

7 Cf. Justin, Apologia I, 66: PG 6, 427; cf. Irenaeus, *Adversus Haereses*, 1.4, c. 18. n. 5: PG 7,1028-1029.

8 S. Congregation of Rites, instruction *Eucharisticum Mysterium*, n. 3a: AAS 59 (1967) 541.

9 Cf. ibid. n. 9, p. 547.

10 Cyril of Jerusalem, Catecheses *Mystagogicae*, V. 21: PG 33, 1126.

11 Cf. Acts 20: 28. and Cf. II Vatican Council, decree *Christus Dominus*, n. 38, 4: AAS 58 (1966) 693.

The Theology of the Fragments **Rich May (2022)**

One of the principle reasons for returning to Communion on the tongue are the fragments that indiscriminately fall from the one distributing Communion and the fragments that are left in the hand of the one receiving the Eucharist. Every fragment, to the smallest, is the Body, Blood, Soul, and Divinity of Jesus Christ.

How large must a fragment of the Eucharist be before we can make the spiritually crucial judgment: Here is the Real Presence of Jesus Christ?

What can be called the "Doctrine of the Fragments" is a corollary of transubstantiation. Jesus Christ remains present in the fragments, the ultimate in divine condescension. A crumb, a drop (*Pie pellicane, Iesu Domine, me immundum munda tuo sanguine; cuius una stilla salvum facere totum mundum quit ab omni scelere* (from *Adoro Te Devote*) ... and the risk? Today these fragments are needlessly neglected or casually abused. It is a matter that lies at the heart of much of our present eucharistic problematics.

St. Thomas Aquinas expressed the position of earlier centuries in this limpid stanza of his *Lauda Sion*: *Fracto demum sacramento ne vacilles, sed memento tantum esse sub fragmento ...* (Nor a single doubt retain, when they break the Host in twain, but that in each part remain what was in the whole before ...)

St Ephrem: *"That which I now give you, do not judge to be brave, take, eat this bread, do not tread upon its crumbs: what I have called my body, this truly is. A particle with its crumbs is able to sanctify thousands of thousands."* (from his Hymni et sermones, IV, 4)

St Cyril of Jerusalem: *"Partake of it, but be sure, not to lose any of it. For if you lose any of it you would clearly suffer a loss, as it were of your own limbs. Tell me, if anyone gave you gold dust, would you not take hold of it with every possible care, ensuring that you would not drop any of it or suffer any loss? So will you not be more cautious to ensure that not a crumb falls away from that which is more precious than gold or more precious than stones?"* (Catechesis mystagogica V. 21-22, Pg 33)

Similar quotes can be found at the **Council of Florence** (*Decretum ad Armmentos*), and also **the Council of Trent:** *"For Christ is all and entire of the form of bread under any part of that form; likewise, the whole Christ is present under the form of bread and wine and under all its parts ... and anyone should deny that in the venerable sacrament of the Eucharist the whole Christ is contained under each form, and under every part of each form, one separated, anathema, sit."*

But even in more recent times, confirmed by the Magisterium:

Paul VI (*Mysterium Fidei*). "In fact, the faithful thought themselves guilty, and rightfully so, if after they receive the body of the Lord, in order to preserve it with all care and reverence, a small fragment of it fell through negligence" (cites Origen, In Exodum, fragment, PG 12, 391).

And then we have M.D. which was discussed above, after citing St. Cyril:

"Further, the practice which must be considered traditional (Communion on the tongue) ensures more effectively that Holy Communion is distributed with proper respect, decorum and dignity. It removes the danger of profanation of the sacred species, in which in a unique way, Christ, God, and Man, is present whole and entire, substantially and continually' ..." (*Eucharisticum Mysterium*, n. 9).

Then there is the Congregation for Divine Worship in their letters to Episcopal Conferences ... "Whatever be the form (of distribution) adopted, care must be taken not to let fall or scatter fragments of the eucharistic bread ..."

There is also the statement from the CDF, May 2, 1973: After Communion the particles that have fallen from the Hosts be reverently preserved or consumed as in the case of the paten. Such instruction is also found in *Immensae Caritatis,* Jan. 25, 1973. The particles include pieces, broken off from the integral, original Host. How small? Fragments and pieces that are still discernible by our senses; bits and tiny pieces visibly seen, fragments that are easily discernible on a paten … *and also visible in your hand ... the same fragments the priest tends to on the altar.* Scrupulosity can be an issue, but is hardly the dominant fault today. One does a careful purification – no visible residue. There have been erroneous theologies, such as that of Karl Rahner, whose emphasis on "sign value" create judgments that became subjective but these must prescind from the objective reality; a discussion beyond the scope of this paper.

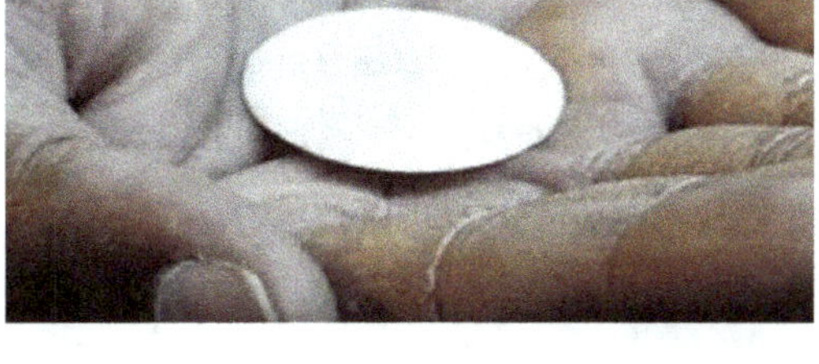

Where do the particles go that are left in the communicant's hand?
Following the guidelines of M.D., does our catechesis communicate this risk and, at a minimum, instruct one to check one's hand for these particles?

Cardinal Robert Sarah

The former Prefect of the Congregation for Divine Worship, Cardinal Robert Sarah, wrote a beautiful defense of the doctrine of the fragments in the preface to Fr. Federico Bortoli's 2018 thesis on canon law (published as "The Distribution of Communion on the Hand: Historical, Juridical, and Pastoral Profiles," Cantagalli, Siena, 2018). He stated:

"We now see how faith in the Real Presence can influence the way of receiving Communion, and vice-versa. Receiving Communion on the hand undoubtedly involves a great dispersion of fragments; whereas paying attention to the smallest crumbs, taking care in purifying the sacred vessels, not touching the Host with sweaty hands – all of these become tiny professions of faith in the Real Presence of Jesus, even in the smallest parts of the consecrated species. If Jesus is the substance of the Eucharistic Bread, and if the dimensions of the fragments are only accidents of the Bread, it matters little whether a piece of the Host is large or small. The substance is the same! It is Him!

On the contrary, inattention to the fragments makes one lose sight of the dogma: little by little the thought begins to prevail: "If even the parish priest does not pay attention to the fragments, if he administers Communion in such a way that the fragments can be dispersed, then either it means that Jesus is not truly present in them, or that he is only "up until a certain point." "Why do we persist in receiving Communion standing and in the hand? Why is there this attitude of a lack of submission to the signs of God? May no priest dare to pretend to impose his own authority on this question, refusing or mistreating those who desire to receive Communion kneeling and on the tongue: let's come like children and receive the Body of Christ humbly, kneeling and on the tongue."

2023, 2025 Photos of fragments from the floor where communion is distributed; later consumed from the cloth.

Most Rev. Bishop Athanasius Schneider:

... if the Eucharist, which contains the Body of Christ, is the most precious treasure, it is at the same time the most fragile and defenseless reality, therefore requiring the utmost care not to lose the smallest fragment, and to avoid the danger of profanation and theft. *The practice of receiving Communion, directly in the hand, undeniably, exposes the Body of Christ – as proven by the facts, established in newspapers around the world,* [confirmed in author's own parish, figure above], *to a considerable loss of Eucharistic fragments to being walked upon, and it also facilitates the theft of sacred Hosts. Can we remain indifferent any longer to these facts? For a soul who truly loves the Lord, should these facts not appear truly horrible?* (Laise, p. ii)

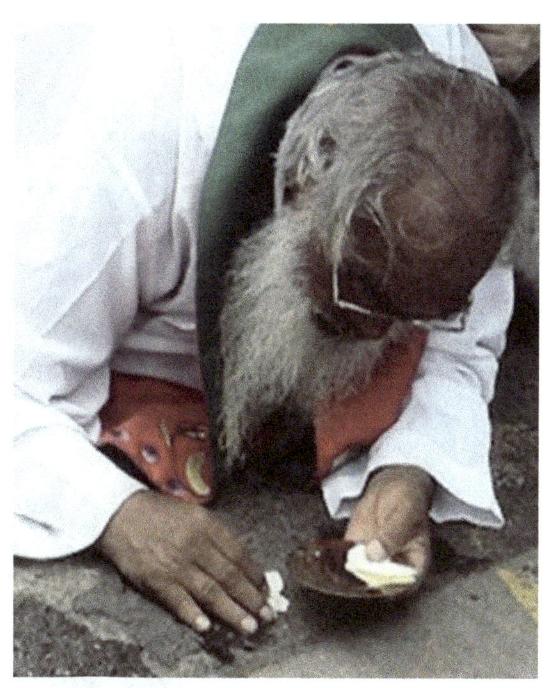

Priest taking it on himself to collect the fragments after distributing Communion. Carpeted floors are even more problematic, trapping the fragments.

Why not return to the safer, more sacred manner, practiced for more than a millennium, receiving the Body of Christ directly on the tongue, thus avoiding the scattering, and significantly reduce cases of theft of sacred Hosts?

Why not return with docility to observing the ardent admonition of Pope Paul VI, namely, of preserving throughout the entire Church, the traditional form of the rite of Holy Communion: ... "This form of distributing Holy Communion should be preserved everywhere, considering the present situation in the Church" and in M.D. 1969 the Apostolic See vehemently urges bishops, priests and faithful to carefully observe the valid and newly confirmed law [of receiving directly on the tongue]?

All possible arguments in favor of continuing with the practice of receiving the Body of Christ standing and in the hand, lose their consistency before these objectively, serious, and often horrible facts, as those of scattering of Eucharistic fragments, of theft of the sacred Hosts, and the blurring of the sacred, sublime and solemn aspects of Holy Communion.

The ultimate fate of most of the fragments of our Lord's Body and Blood.

References by Topic:

Introduction

(Ref 1P5 https://onepeterfive.com/communion-hand-true-story/*Originally published at La Nuova Bussola Quotidiana. Originally reprinted at 1P5 on May 8, 2018. Translated by Giuseppe Pellegrino).* Accessed 21 Jan 2023.

A. History

Msgr. Nicola Bux, Communion in the Hand (Parts 1-3) ... https://newdailycompass.com/en/communion-in-the-hand-legitimised-disobedience, accessed 30 Jan 2023. [All 3 parts can be reviewed in publication by Preserving Christian Publications: "Communion in the Hand Disobedience Permitted." Msgr. Nicola Bux. https://www.pcpbooks.net/buxeng.html. Accessed Feb 1, 2023.

"History of Communion on the Hand," Northern Cross Apologetics Catechesis, September 2021. https://www.stelizabethjulian.org/a-history-of-communion-on-the-hand.html. Accessed 28 Jan 2023.

Luisella Scrosatim, "The True Story of Communion in the Hand;" 1P5 https://onepeterfive.com/communion-hand-true-story/*Originally published at La Nuova Bussola Quotidiana. Originally reprinted at 1P5 on May 8, 2018. Translated by Giuseppe Pellegrino*); Accessed Jan 29, 2023.

Laise, *Communion in the Hand,* p, ii, iii, 1-5, 19, 97, 99.

Catholic Register, "Why Communion on the Tongue is More Suitable than in the Hand". https://www.ncregister.com/blog/why-communion-on-the-tongue-is-more-suitable-than-in-the-hand?amp&gclid=EAIaIQobChMI692zlc3y_AIVGi-tBh3TcgpSEAMYASAAEgI45vD_BwE. Accessed Feb 8, 2023.

B. Issue of Reverence

Laise, *Communion in the Hand*, p. ii

1P5 https://onepeterfive.com/communion-hand-true-story/*Originally published at La Nuova Bussola Quotidiana. Originally reprinted at 1P5 on May 8, 2018. Translated by Giuseppe Pellegrino.* Accessed Jan 29, 2023.

C. Theology of the Fragments

Rev. Richard W. Gilsdorf , "The Doctrine of the Fragments," Homiletic and Pastoral Review, Feb. 1980.

Laise, *Communion in the Hand*, pp. ii, 100.

Bux, *Communion in the Hand* (Part 2). https://www.pcpbooks.net/buxeng.html. Accessed Feb 1, 2023.

Luisella Scrosatim, The True Story of Communion in the Hand; 1P5 https://onepeterfive.com/communion-hand-true-story/*Originally published at La Nuova Bussola Quotidiana. Originally reprinted at 1P5 on May 8, 2018. Translated by Giuseppe Pellegrino)*

https://newdailycompass.com/en/communion-in-the-hand-legitimised-disobedience

Chapter 7

Having the courage to kneel. True stories:

Story one

The sister of a friend of mine came into town to visit. She was told that the nearest church in her part of town is where they prohibit kneeling. Short for time, with no options, she went anyway. Her stress level rose as she proceeded in the communion line and got to the front. She decided to kneel anyway. She was asked to stand up. Her response: "But this is God!" She was given Communion anyway.

Story two

I had been receiving communion on the tongue for many years, but never on my knees because of my position in a communion line and no kneeler. However, finally, at one Mass, the person in front of me kneeled. This gave. me the courage to go ahead and kneel. And I've been kneeling ever since.

Story three

I have been told for sometime that most people don't care to kneel anyway, and are happy in the communion line standing. Acting as an acolyte at a hospital chapel, I had gone ahead and purchased a kneeler and paten. Attendance at this Mass was usually between 20 and 25 people with four or five kneeling on the floor during Communion. Finally, it was time for its trial run. The kneeler was put in place in front of the altar and was pulled out just before Communion with an acting server using the paten. Without prompting anyone, the number of people kneeling went to 18. This reveals an important point that when the kneeler is there, people <u>will</u> kneel. A few were unable or preferred not to kneel, but were still able to stand, holding their hand out for Communion in the hand or on the tongue. This just reinforces the fact that one can stand or kneel with the kneeler in place. Communicants were reminded to check for fragments in the hand.

O Jesus, present in the Sacrament of the Altar,
teach all nations to serve you with a willing heart,
knowing that to serve God is to reign.
May your sacrament, O Jesus,
be light to the mind,
strength to the will,
joy to the heart.
May it be the support for the weak,
the comfort for the suffering,
the wayfaring bread of salvation for the dying,
and, for all, the pledge of future glory.

Pope St. John XXIII

Chapter 8 Communion in the Hand … Answering the Objections
Ref: Juan Rodolfo Laise [1]

1) It is only a return to the original practice

Laise: Since this argument is widely disseminated, this false rationale needs to be handled in detail (Chapter 8). Communion in the hand does not bring us closer to the sources of the primitive church, but rather to Protestantism and many current doctoral deviations.

Comments:
The new practice of Communion in the hand would NOT truly be a "rediscovery" of an "ancient tradition ... returning to the reception of Communion as it was done in the early Church by the early Church Fathers" as one often hears said. In general, resorting to the "primitive church" does not always apply and ignores the organic development within the Church. For example, administration of Confession (Penance) in the early Church was a public matter, sinners confessed their sins publicly before the assembled faithful. Should we return to that? *Primitivism* has its flaws, ignores the Church's continual advancement, through the power of the Holy Spirit - Christ, acting in his Church as time goes on.

So -- **What about Communion in the hand in the early Church?**

It was terminated by the 10th century. Why? *"From early papal writings, Communion in the hand was stopped not only primarily to prevent desecration, but also primarily because of heresies against the Real Presence –* ***a conscious, deliberate weakening of faith in the Real Presence."*** (See resources)

Msgr. Laise expresses the conviction that the Gospel of John, the writings of the early Fathers, and also the Syrian ("Codex Purpureus Rossanensis") of Rossano (5th century) all demonstrate instead that Jesus gave Communion to the Apostles on the tongue.

In the Instruction *Memoriale Domini* it says clearly that, although in early Christianity this ***feeling of reverence towards this Sacrament and a deeper humility was felt to be demanded when receiving it. Thus the custom was established of the minister placing the particle of the Sacred Species on the tongue of the communicant." Thus it was that, at a certain time, one practice replaced the other, to the point that the earlier practice was not only abandoned but even explicitly prohibited.***

From this context it is clearly seen that, for Pope Paul VI, this change of practice constituted an imperfect form from a more perfect form of reception.
In fact, the ancient texts never say that the Fathers of the Church found any advantage in giving Communion on the hand, nor that they ever praised this practice in itself. The texts simply describe it was the only way of receiving Communion that was known at that time. Indeed, as Msgr. Laise says, the Fathers' frequent warnings about the dangers linked to it reveal the imperfection inherent in this way of receiving Communion. Therefore, Laise believes that although Communion in the hand was certainly the practice of the ancient Fathers, they would have desired to receive Communion on the tongue [had they been given the option].

Many centuries later, the practice of Communion in the hand, which was "neutral" in the Patristic era, was adopted by the Protestant reformers with a clear doctrinal connotation. For example, according to Martin Bucer, a promoter of the Anglican "reform," the practice of not giving Communion in the hand is a rejection of two [Catholic] "superstitions" – the "false honor" that is claimed to be attributed to this Sacrament and the "perverse belief" that the hands of the ministers are more holy than the hands of the laity as a result of the anointing they receive in the rite of Ordination. From this moment on, the act of receiving Communion in the hand has a markedly polemical significance of being opposed to Communion on the tongue as the expression of an opposing doctrine in two fundamental points that distinguish Protestant belief from Catholic: the Real Presence and the priesthood. This implication cannot be ignored.

… when the practice of Communion in the hand began to spread in Catholic circles in the second half of the 20th Century, it was not a mere return to an ancient custom. Thus it is no coincidence that precisely in one of the first places where Communion in the hand was abusively introduced, a "*New Catechism*" was published shortly before (the famous "*Dutch Catechism*"), to which the Holy See was forced to make numerous modifications (14 major, 45 minor) to correct grave doctrinal errors. In this text, commissioned by the Dutch bishops and presented through a "collective pastoral letter," the real and substantial presence of Christ in the Eucharist was placed in doubt, an inadmissible explanation of transubstantiation was given, *and any form whatsoever of the presence of Jesus Christ in the particles or broken fragments of the Host after the Consecration was denied.* In addition, the … *Dutch Catechism* causes confusion about the difference between the common priesthood of the baptized and the hierarchical priesthood of the ordained.

2) The practice does not have to do with the essence of the sacrament, but with the changeable part of it

Laise: Even these changes cannot be carried out arbitrarily, but rather in a homogeneous matter.

3) It is more in keeping with the dignity of the Christian and corresponds to the stage of adulthood

Laise: *Memoriale Domini* states it is indispensable to receive the Eucharist with humility, and this was precisely one of the reasons for starting Communion on the tongue. The dignity of a Christian is already sufficiently emphasized by the fact of being able to receive Communion, the Body and Blood of our Lord; and on the tongue does not take away from the dignity of the person.

4) Greater awareness of the common priesthood.

Laise: The common priesthood is already sufficiently expressed by participating in the liturgy and receiving Communion, something only a baptized person can do. An exaggerated reception of the common priesthood is very widespread, which ignores the essential distinction between it and a ministerial priesthood.

5) The theme of the importance of the body; "the hand is as worthy as the mouth"

Laise: Strictly speaking, all parts of the body have the same dignity, but nonetheless, no one doubts that in any culture, there are parts of the body that are considered noble and others that are not; there are shameful parts. No one would think of placing one's feet or sitting in places that are considered holy. We're not comparing the hands of the faithful with their mouth, but rather the hands of the faithful with those of the priest who is specifically anointed to touch the body of the Lord. We have the profane and we have the consecrated. Mixing the profane with the consecrated is an issue in and of itself, which includes the consecrated vessels.

6) The significance of the gesture

Laise: ... the gesture as a sign. The gesture of receiving the Eucharist in the hand in antiquity had no special meaning. For the Protestant, the presence of Christ was not real and substantial, and the priest was not different from the layman. In the 1960s, it signifies the rebellion against the authority of the pope. From the concession of the indult one should be careful to note that it does not signify anything of this nature, but rather what was indicated by the pastoral letter, n.3 (accompanies *Memoriale Domini*).

7) Active participation

Laise: The Council says that part of the "active participation" is to keep a sacred silence at the appropriate time. For this the hands folded, we could say, "quiet" far from being an inert attitude, are an eloquent sign of the "humility ... demanded when receiving [this sacrament]."

8) Respect for the freedom of the faithful

Laise: This is not a reason to introduce the change. This liberty is only a consequence of the change already introduced. The possibility of freely electing requires objective information. If we are to propose to the faithful the choice without warning them of the dangers that this could bring about, the resistance of the pope to approve it, and his absolute preference for the traditional practice. On the contrary, if we were to allow an enormous "propaganda" in favor of the new practice, we would not be giving them the opportunity of a free decision; "only the truth will set you free."

9) The rite is not so important; the important thing is the faith

Laise: The documents of the time indicate that Paul VI did not consider the rite to be indifferent. The pope considered the possibility of introducing Communion in the hand with "evident apprehension" and thought the matter was "one of the most sensitive and urgent" ... a "matter … so serious in itself with its consequences, " and he called for "the mature reflection required by so serious a matter," and considered the practice "in itself not contrary to doctrine but a practice very debatable and dangerous in practice."

10) It is more in keeping with contemporary sensitivities with respect to hygiene

Laise: This has no support and tradition or the Magisterium. It appeared among the arguments of those who were in favor … [and in the] questions sent to the bishops in 1968, but is not even mentioned in M.D., which proves that it was considered to be of little importance. [There was a presumed danger of transmitting sickness, which can only be avoided by forbidding Communion on the tongue]. In fact, the transmission of sickness by receiving Communion in the hand, touched by the fingers of the Extraordinary Eucharistic Minister, can equally transmit sickness.

Comment: COVID appears to have run its course. There is the objection for Communion on the tongue because it increases the risk of infection. Interestingly enough, a groundbreaking study in May 2021 debunks this widespread misconception that administering Holy Communion in the hand and standing is safer than dispensing the Sacred Host on the tongue while kneeling. This fear goes against the best available scientific evidence, which appears in *The Journal of Religion and Health.*[2] Kneeling separates vertically the head of the one distributing with the one kneeling where the transmission of germs is most likely.

11) The sign value of the liturgy, so as to comply better with the Lord's command: "Take and eat, this is my Body"

Laise: It is to force the text if one wants to see expressed there in the action of "take" to be in the hand. In the manner of Semitic expression, it is most frequent that a preceding or concomitant action be explicit.

12) The fundamental sense of the ecclesiastical. Since many countries have accepted the two praxes, to revert to Communion on the tongue will cause confusion

Laise: Had the "fundamental sense of the ecclesiastical" been kept in mind from the beginning, the Episcopal Conferences would have heard the vehement exhortation of Pope Paul VI to diligently submit and reaffirm to keep the law in force. Keeping in mind the common good of the Church, the practice would not have spread. The fundamental sense of the ecclesiastical is what was lacking in those who imposed Communion in the hand.

---

1 Most Rev. Juan Rodolfo Laise, *Holy Communion* (Boonville, N.Y., Preserving Christian Publications, 2018) 36, 37, 44-45, 57-59, 92-97. Not precise quotes.

2 *The Journal of Religion and Health,* also the NLM – Report that the dangers are minimal, even when drinking from the cup. See: https://pmc.ncbi.nlm.nih.gov/articles/PMC7377019/ . Accessed June 6, 2025.

Chapter 10

Typical portable kneeler layouts

<u>Option One</u> Multiple Kneelers in a row

One priest, or with deacon, with servers/patens

Even in large churches, people cross through the pews to the two center aisles and return from the side.

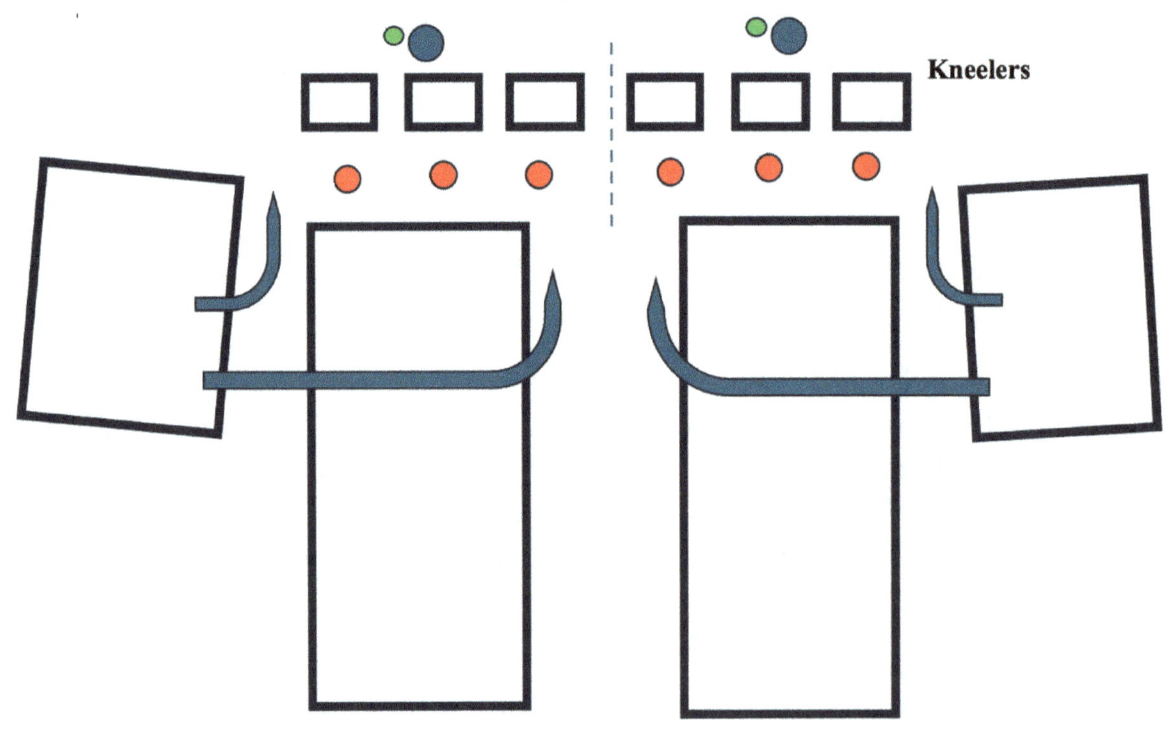

<u>Option Two</u> Two Kneelers

Similar to option one …
Two priests or priest with deacon, with two servers/patens.
Can work in large churches … As in option one, people again cross through the pews to the center aisle returning from the side.

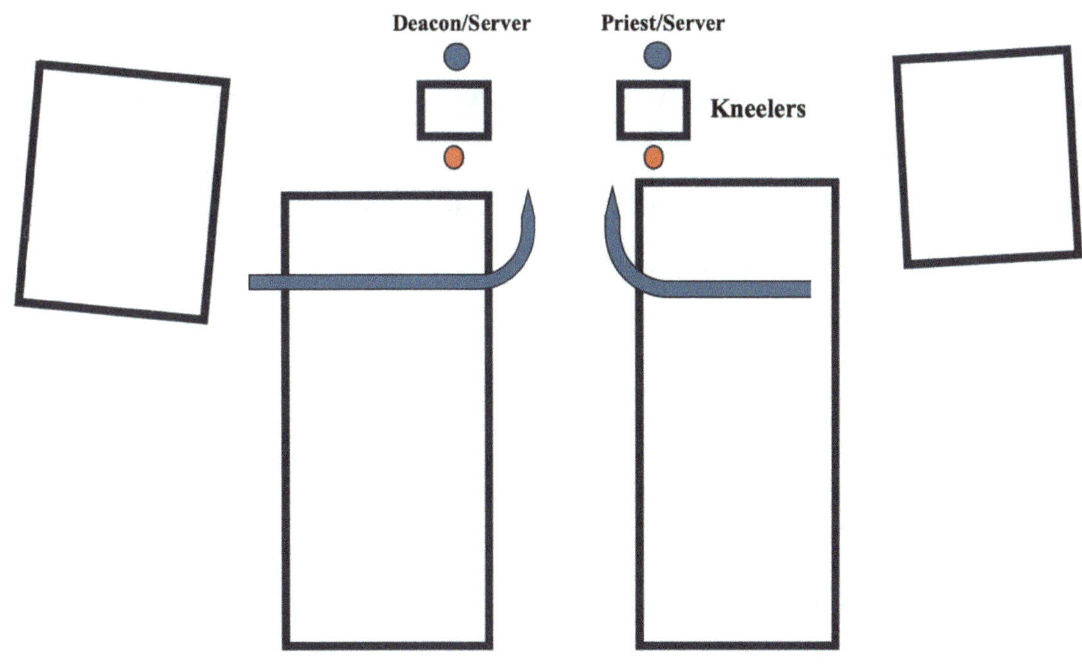

Selected Bibliography

***Catechism of the Catholic Church,* Libreria Editrice Vaticana, 1992.**

Bergsma, John. *Jesus and the Dead Sea Scrolls,* New York: Image, 2019.

Flannery, John O.P. Austin. *Vatican Council II: The Conciliar and Postconciliar Documents* (Rev. edition). Collegeville, Mn.: Liturgical Press, 1996.

Gamber, Msgr. Klaus. *The Reform of the Roman Liturgy, Its Problems and Background.* Fort Collins, CO: Roman Catholic Books, 1993.

Jurgens, William A. *The Faith of the Early Fathers. Vol 1.* Collegeville, Minnesota: Liturgical Press, 1970.

Keating, Karl. *Catholicism and Fundamentalism.* San Francisco: Ignatius Press, 1988.

Kwasniewski, Dr. Peter. *The Holy Bread of Eternal Life, Restoring Eucharistic Reverence in an age of Impiety.* (Manchester, N.H: Sophia Institute Press, 2020.

Laise, Most Rev. Juan Rodolfo. *Holy Communion.* Boonville, N.Y.: Preserving Christian Publications, 2020.

Ratzinger, Joseph Cardinal. *The Spirit of the Liturgy*. San Francisco: Ignatius Press, 2010.

Reid, Alcuin O.S.B, *The Organic Development of the Liturgy*. San Francisco: Ignatius Press, 2005.

Sarah, Cardinal Robert. *The Day is Now Far Spent.* San Francisco: Ignatius Press, 2019.

Sarah, Cardinal Robert. *The Power of Silence*. San Francisco: Ignatius Press, 2017.

Sofie, Rev. J. Francis ,OP, *Martyrs of the Eucharist: Stories to Inspire Eucharistic Amazement.* Rockford, Ill: Tan Books, 2024.

The Church Music Association of America. *The Parish Book of Chant.* Richmond, Virginia: CMAA, 2008.

Tucker, Jeffery. *Sing Like a Catholic*. Richmond Virginia: The Church Music Association of America, 2009.

United States Conference of Catholic Bishops. *United States Catholic Catechism for Adults,* 2006.

www.ingramcontent.com/pod-product-compliance
Lightning Source LLC
LaVergne TN
LVHW061248100826
845148LV00008B/1063

* 9 7 9 8 8 8 8 7 0 4 4 3 1 *